Dying Well

A HOLISTIC GUIDE
FOR THE DYING AND
THEIR CARERS

Spend your brief moment according to nature's law,
and serenely greet the journey's end as an olive falls
when it is ripe, blessing the branch that bore it,
and giving thanks to the tree that gave it life.

MARCUS AURELIUS

Dying Well

A HOLISTIC GUIDE
FOR THE DYING AND
THEIR CARERS

Richard Reoch

RESOURCE *Publications* · Eugene, Oregon

Resource Publications
A division of Wipf and Stock Publishers
199 W 8th Ave, Suite 3
Eugene, OR 97401

Dying Well
A Holistic Guide for the Dying and Their Causes
By Reoch, Richard and Menuhin, Yehudi
Copyright © 1997 by Reoch, Richard All rights reserved.
ISBN-13: 9781725268159
Publication date 3/2/2020
Previously published by Gaia Books Limited, 1997

This edition is a scanned facsimile of the original edition published in 1997.

Contents

Foreword

Dying, as a leaf in autumn, its life fully served, at last a riot of burning colour, depleted of vital energies, as if it were a final immolation to beauty – the disembodied leaf is blown earthwards to enable the following year's growth to be nourished and healthy, to complete the cycle from darkness to light, from earth to sun.

Such glorious dying may still be found among matured human beings, fully conscious of a completed personal term essential to the continuity of all life. My mother left us in a death most benign. She had reached the ripe age of two months short of 101, had been in full possession of her faculties, although, unfortunately, she had fallen some years before and was dependent on a walker and her hearing was failing; but her thinking was acute and alert. She was fully composed and laughed with the happy abandon of a young person who knew enough of sadness and of unfulfilled longing to become wise and patient.

Preparation for death used to be cultivated among the holy men of India and Tibet, and the Tibetan Book of the Dead gives elaborate instructions to the dying and to those near them. It was thus that Aldous Huxley died, in peace, as his beloved wife Laura read to him.

Today we can hardly claim that the majority of people prepare or are prepared for death. The human curses of hate and envy, of untimely death due to disease, war, the ambitions of tyrants and politicians, or due to famine, torture and to broken hearts or deranged thoughts are nightmares of suffering. All of these circumstances cause deaths that can only be bitter. But some of these tragic deaths might at least be mitigated.

Of course, we should first look at man himself: abused, ignorant, by definition a religious animal, exercising free choice, often against his will and his talents – for his life is at most times tailored to his ambitions, his imaginings and his fears. These can be life-enhancing but, when ill-directed, suicidal.

Let us, therefore, concern ourselves with early meditation on the subject of life and death, with poetry and music, revealing, inspiring and moving, so that our children may lead a balanced, healthy and long life. The foundations of such a life should be laid in the earliest years with singing, dancing, with examples and opportunities which would subtly mould the raw and brutal into the expression of art in *life*, in our every activity, and finally in death.

Let the dying help the living all their lives, for we are on the road to achieving the full potential of our senses, our talents, our intellect, our dreams and our faith, as we live and die simultaneously – for all of us are ignorant – on a hopefully circuitous road to death, even as we are born.

This book is meant to make death easier for those who have been granted a little time or who may, in the full blossom of their power, wish to think ahead with a little foresight. May it be inspiring to the dying as well as to the "carers" and contribute to a more general familiarity with this essential law of nature. May it enhance the respect we owe life, *all* life, at *all* stages.

YEHUDI MENUHIN

Introduction

Throughout human culture there has been a sustained tradition of people who looked death steadfastly in the face, embraced it and died well. In doing so they transformed their own lives and the lives of all who knew them.

Now, more than ever, we need to listen to the wisdom of that remarkable tradition and its priceless legacy. In an era which has sought inexorably to eliminate awareness of death, first through denial and then through institutionalization, the time has come to re-think fundamentally our approach to dying.

About this book

This book aims to be of help to three groups of readers:
• people confronted with terminal illnesses or life-threatening conditions
• people who are caring for dying people or looking for new ways to support friends who are dying
• people who are seeking advice on how they can prepare for death and use the encounter with their own mortality to benefit themselves, their families and friends.

Drawing on the lessons learned from the contemporary revolution in attitudes towards childbirth, this book shows how openness, advance planning and the use of complementary health therapies can benefit dying people.

It examines the emotional storm and suggests ways in which understanding and preparing for death can transform our loves and relationships.

To compile this work, Gaia Books has drawn extensively on the experience of medical specialists, psychologists, counsellors and other carers working in hospices and with the dying.

What makes the advice in this book unique is that it gives particular emphasis to the practical possibilities offered by a range of complementary therapies which can enable families and loved ones to support both each other and those for whom they are caring. All the herbs and flower essences, and the exercises and massage techniques throughout the book have been included under the direct supervision of leading authors and teachers in these fields.

The art of living well and the art of dying well are one.

EPICURUS

Breaking through

More and more people are coming to the conclusion that we have gone seriously astray in our approach to dying. For many people this breakthrough begins with the shock of finding themselves almost completely unprepared when they are faced either with their own death or with the death of someone they love.

They are unable to exercise effective control in discussions with doctors, friends and family. They are unable to cope with the storm of turbulent and powerful emotions that rise up within them. They find a terrible abyss widening between themselves and those closest to them. They fear being alone, yet feel more alone than ever before in their lives.

After death the commercial funeral industry takes over. A staggering profit is made out of services that were once freely provided by the community. Sadly, in all too many cases, family and friends find that their innermost needs have been left unanswered.

A new understanding

The need to reassess our approach to dying is increasingly acknowledged. The hospice movement has challenged conventional hospital procedures. Doctors and others caring for the dying have begun to speak out, calling for a new understanding and a new approach to caring. Environmental protection groups have started to propose alternatives to wasteful and toxic funeral practices.

It is in this spirit that this book has been compiled. It is not a set of prescriptions. It offers alternative approaches. The advice and therapies in these pages may help you understand, clarify or even change your attitudes, but no moral judgment is passed on other ways of dying. You may find some treatments very helpful for yourself or those for whom you are caring. Ultimately, the decision to experiment with them is yours. This book will have served its purpose well if it reminds you that you are free to make that decision.

Dying well

The idea of dying well is sometimes mistaken for dying in our sleep, slipping away under heavy sedatives or lying back and feeling good while the body gives up the ghost.

Such might be the ideals of some, but dying well involves a fuller understanding of death, a conscious application of its lessons in our lives. It involves cultivating the attitudes and feelings by which both the dying person and those around them can live out the fullness of their humanity.

Dying well does not mean dying a "good death". The very phrase conjures up the notion of a perfect, romanticized death. As with all fantasies, you can do yourself great harm by trying to impose it on your actual experience.

Appropriate death

More helpful is the concept of an "appropriate death". This is a way of dying that reflects, as far as possible, your own personality and values. What matters, from this viewpoint, is not other people's stereotyped views of good and bad deaths, but the nature of your own experience.

The US psychiatrist Avery Weisman wrote: "Obviously, appropriate death for one person might be unsuitable for another. What might seem appropriate from the outside might be utterly meaningless to the dying person himself. Conversely, deaths that seem unacceptable to an outsider, might be desirable from the inner viewpoint of the patient."

Some deaths clearly fall outside this framework. Events around the world teach us daily that the full spectrum of human experience includes death under many circumstances – in sudden accidents, disasters and violent attacks, in war or under torture. Many deaths appear senseless, yet all ultimately have an unfolding significance. Every death also highlights our own mortality and underlines the fundamental importance of understanding that reality in our lives.

Let us deprive death of its strangeness, let us frequent it, let us get used to it; let us have nothing more often in mind than death. We do not know where death awaits us; so let us wait for it everywhere. To practise death is to practise freedom. A person who has learned how to die has unlearned how to be a slave.

MONTAIGNE

The death storm

At the eye of the death storm is some of the most profound emotional turbulence that a human being can experience. What lies at the root of this pain and why are we so ill-equipped to recognize it and deal with it? What is necessary to transform fear into courage, anger into insight and denial into rediscovery?

The following parts of this book examine the emotional and other dimensions of dying and introduce complementary therapy techniques that help the experience of death to become a precious period of interpersonal warmth and support.

PART ONE, *Nature's way*, presents the holistic approach to the care of the dying and offers fundamental exercises for both mind and body that can be used at various stages by dying people and their carers.

PART TWO, *Loving and caring*, focuses on the application of a range of complementary health therapies in the care of the dying person.

PART THREE, *The great storm*, looks at the emotional stresses involved in the encounter with death, examines the roots of those feelings in our daily lives, and how they affect communication between dying people, their carers and friends.

PART FOUR, *Giving and letting go*, explores ways in which dying people can discover their potential for generosity, forgiveness and personal transformation.

PART FIVE, *The return journey*, explores the needs of bereavement, grief and remembrance, offers support for those affected by unexpected and young deaths and includes an extensive Resource section for further information and help.

At each stage, readers are offered a series of trigger questions to stimulate reflection on their lives at the present time. In this way, death is used as a powerful mirror to play its spiritual role of adviser and guide in the midst of life.

Throughout Asia in the early morning people bring flowers to their temples, reciting these words as remembrance of their own transience:

We offer flowers that today are fresh and sweetly blooming, Flowers that tomorrow will be faded and fallen. Our bodies too, like flowers, fade and pass away.

Preparing for birth, preparing for death

Death is psychologically as important as birth. Shrinking away from it is something unhealthy and abnormal which robs the second half of life of its purpose.

CARL G. JUNG

Two profound transformations determine the course of our lives: one is our birth, the other is our death. Both are moments of great change.

Both fill us with awesome feelings. They call up thoughts and emotions that we glimpse only rarely in our ordinary experience. We are in the presence of the miraculous and the mysterious.

The lessons of "natural childbirth" have been learned. Today, increasing numbers of parents are taking positive and caring control of the birth process, rather than treating it as a medical crisis. We are only now starting to apply that wisdom to dying well.

What makes a birth unhappy and painful can be just as true for the experience of dying. Both are moments of supreme vulnerability. Yet by understanding more about these moments, and the steps we can take to influence them, it is possible for great pain to co-exist with – and even be transformed by – tenderness, compassion and insight.

Preparing for birth and death involves similar psychological, physical and social processes. For example, studies have shown that an invisible environment of assumptions and feelings radically affects even the pain of childbirth. If the mother is treated as "ill", or made to feel fearful, anxious or humiliated, the pain may be all-consuming. But warmth, openness and the physical and emotional support of close friends have been shown to be more powerful pain-relievers than some conventional drugs. The same scenario – and solution – surrounds the dying person.

There is no uniform, ideal birth. Each birth is unique. It is possibly the most intense experience shared by mother, father and child. For the parents, the birth process can be seen as a voyage in which both encounter their own intense emotions and inner powers.

Recent studies of "birthing" stressed the importance to the parents of retaining a measure of understanding and decision-making throughout the entire process, even at moments of great pain. Many aspects of childbearing which were once not openly discussed have now been opened up. Matters that were previously left solely to the professionals are the subject of childbirth classes. Husbands, partners and "birthing friends" are now included in the preparation for and in the actual process of giving birth. Such enlightenment has now dawned in the world of caring for the dying.

Physical contact and touch are among the most powerful forms of support that can be given to those faced with uncertainty, fear and pain. Touching, massage and holding have been termed the "anchor in the stormy sea of labour". This is also the experience of those working with the dying, who recognize in these forms of human contact a way of saying to the dying "I care about you. You mean far more to me than I can express."

Both birth and death carry with them high degrees of unpredictability, and it would be a serious mistake either for a prospective mother or someone with a terminal illness to think that there is a magic formula for pain-free births or deaths. Yet it is possible, by exercising greater responsibility for the course of these events, to retain a measure of intelligent involvement in decision-making and to develop a realistic acceptance of the physical and psychological transformations that occur.

Ageing and growing

Our fear of death is intimately bound up with our attitude towards ageing. There has always been a romantic dream of eternal youth, but in many countries today this has developed into a collective obsession. A healthy reaction against this neurosis is now emerging as people start to question the all-pervasive stereotypes of youth and the corresponding social prejudice against older people.

One of the most hurtful misconceptions about the process of ageing is the assumption that at some point in their lives people inevitably stop growing personally. This attitude has an insidious effect, like a self-fulfilling prophecy. The result is that older people are all too often treated as if they had already stopped living. They enter a kind of twilight zone. Many simply withdraw into themselves and wither away, or are placed in nursing homes.

But the so-called "grey revolution" is gathering momentum as older people start to attack these attitudes at their roots. They are emerging as an increasingly powerful political force: their numbers are constantly growing as life expectancy goes up, and their purchasing power is outstripping that of the young.

We are citizens of eternity.

FYODOR DOSTOYEVSKY

The potential of life

This resurgence reflects a deeper truth. The later years of life can be transformed into a period of great creativity and personal growth. Energy which was previously concentrated on the demands of work and family life can be channelled into other interests and longings. If this happens, your world expands. You tend to become more generous, caring and courageous. You may be more reflective and self-aware, more in tune with your emotions and deeper aspirations, keenly interested in learning and willing to share your experience with others.

As your sense of the potential of life deepens, your former preconceptions about death begin to change. If it is possible for life to be transformed in this way, you ask yourself, what possibilities are inherent in the experience of dying?

As a tree ages it grows, each year's ring strengthening and adding to its power. In cultures where the process of ageing is respected and supported, people's final years can become ones of continued development. The elders are the living treasures of the community.

There may be a neurological basis for the idea that wisdom comes with old age. Recent research has discovered that some neurons in the area of the brain where higher thought takes place appear to multiply after maturity and that the filaments of many neurons continue to grow in healthy older people.

Attitudes of the elderly

The attitudes of older individuals are as varied as the lives they have led, but in study after study they tell us:

• They do not fear death so much as they fear dying. In the words of one: "The deep-seated anxiety is, am I going to become incontinent, dotty, not able to communicate, and a burden? If I could die with a bit of dignity and not having taken up too much of other people's time, I would be happy."

• They often experience real difficulty in finding somebody willing to listen seriously to them and engage with them in their experience of ageing or dying. (The idea that death is seen to be more "natural" for older people can be misused as an excuse for the inadequate care and resources that our society gives to people in the late years of their lives.)

Beginnings and endings

People who are dying are treated differently to other people. But what do we really mean by the word "dying" and when does that process begin in our lives?

Death is such a fundamental process in nature that, without it, living things could not exist. From the moment of birth the cells of our body are endlessly dying and being replaced. The body that dies is not the body that was born. In order to grow, we experience many deaths. Over and over again we shed our appearance, our attitudes and our behaviour as we change from one stage of life to the next. The person who dies is only one of the people we became as we lived.

Perhaps we have been shocked by the sudden death of someone who lived with a fatal condition for years without knowing it and without having any obvious symptoms. All the time that we knew them, they were living literally on the edge of death. Looking back, we realize that we can never know at what point in their life their dying began.

On the other hand, even after being diagnosed as having a terminal illness, we may continue to live for years. The diagnosis turns out only to be a statement of probability. We continue being both a living person and a dying person at the same time.

As we come to understand more and more about the physiological processes of living and dying, the old distinctions between the two are being eroded. The most advanced investigations of modern science (see "Dying in a changing universe", page 123) point us inexorably towards the words of the Anglican Book of Prayer: "In the midst of life, we are in death." They also tell us that the opposite is equally true: in the midst of death, we are in life.

If we are to go beyond the conventional view of good and bad deaths, we need to ask ourselves if our own fear of death is rooted in an outdated model of life. And we need to ask in what other ways we can view life and death.

Lifelines

Humanity has very different ways of imagining how death unfolds. The first two ways, or lifelines, shown below are linear models in which death is the end of life, involving loss, cessation and pain. The model of an afterlife adds a significant trajectory to linear death. The other three lifelines involve cycles, wave patterns and spirals. Both life and death have very different meanings when seen from those perspectives.

1. *Dust to dust, ashes to ashes.* In the words of one philosopher, life is "nasty, brutish and short". It begins and ends in pain. Death is the annihilation of life and robs existence of meaning.

2. *To everything there is a season.* Each life follows a natural sequence. We are born in Spring, at the height of our powers in Summer, mature in Autumn and in the Winter of our years we decline and die.

3. *Eternal life.* Our life from birth to death is but a brief interlude of suffering, after which we live eternally in realms beyond this world.

4. *The wheel of life.* Our existence is a constant pattern of cyclical change. Life constantly changes into death and each moment of death is a moment of birth. We perceive beginnings and endings, but the flow of existence is never ending.

6. *The ascent of life.* Life forms have different levels of consciousness, but all of them have the potential for evolution. Human beings can manifest this potential to a very high degree. We can become aware of dimensions that transcend our limited understanding of our bodies and minds, and enter into a different experience of life and death.

5. *The wavicle.* Quantum physics has shown that at the sub-atomic level there is no distinction between matter and energy. Both have the qualities of particles and waves, giving rise to the concept of the "wavicle". This discovery radically reinterprets our understanding of "life" and "death". We are perpetual patterns of the energy of the cosmos. What we perceive to be the birth and death of finite individuals is simply the unending movement of the universe.

What can I do?

One of the deepest fears we have about death is dying alone. Yet at the very time when genuine human contact can be of such importance, many people turn away from the dying or have great difficulty in being with them. This awkwardness often continues after the death and can lead to people crossing the road to avoid speaking to the bereaved.

It is worth reflecting on why this happens because it can tell us much about our own response to dying and bereavement. We may also see ways in which to change our own attitudes and behaviour towards dying people, since our habit of turning away can actually make their experience worse.

A close look also tends to expose one of the most damaging stereotypes we have inherited about dying: the idea that death is an alien force that devours us according to an inhuman logic and in whose grip we are helpless. On close examination, we find that the experience of dying differs radically from person to person and that there is much in our own behaviour and attitudes that determines what the quality of our experience will be.

A taboo restrains us

Many people have trouble relating to dying people because the subject of death has been a social taboo for so long. There are many ways in which we continue to live in a death-denying society. Even though every single human being on the planet dies, there is a socially reinforced effort to banish this truth from our midst. The taboo is at work on many levels: the phrases we use to avoid talking about death; the way in which death tends to be treated as a medical crisis and handed over to the professionals; and the social pressures that either cover up death or suppress open discussion of it. Not surprisingly, if death is a taboo subject for us and we deny death, we find ourselves unable to reach out to others. We are unaware of the help we could give and receive from each other.

What is the greatest wonder? Each day death strikes and yet we live as if we were immortal. This is the greatest wonder.

THE MAHABHARATA

The natural limits of life

Medical science has accelerated its quest for the prevention of death. This has dramatically influenced our perception of certain illnesses and how people with terminal conditions should be treated. Each new cure is portrayed in the news media as a step towards the eventual elimination of all causes of death. The development of high-tech medical care has also shifted resources from the long-term care of chronic conditions and elderly people to the short-term crisis management of acute life-threatening conditions. The heroic "never-say-die" approach of much contemporary medicine has created new dilemmas as dying bodies are kept alive by machinery and chemicals.

Recently, there has been a welcome recognition of the need to start treating the whole person, to accept natural limits on the prolongation of people's life functions and to provide them with "palliative care" that focuses on reducing pain and improving their quality of life.

"I don't know what to do or say"

Confronted with the death of someone we know and love, we often find ourselves at a complete loss to know what to do or say. We are not even sure what to think and are often unable to comprehend what we really feel. This shock is partly natural, but it is also partly the result of living in a human environment in which we have become de-skilled in dealing with death. Because death is not talked about but handed over to specialists instead, we have very little experience of dealing with it ourselves. Without this experience, and without strong religious or other enduring values which are often hard to define in the context of contemporary society, we are unprepared for the spiritual crisis engendered by our encounter with death. We are inwardly paralysed. We are not necessarily turning away from those in need, we simply do not know what to do.

The alternative tradition

*"Like a petal dropping in the morning sunlight and
floating serenely to the earth, so must the wise prepare
themselves for death, silent and inwardly unmoved."*

So ran the timeless advice imparted to the Samurai,
the illustrious spiritual warriors of Classical Japan.

Trained for death at any moment, these fearless
swordsmen, poets and artists chose for the symbol of
their lineage the fragile cherry blossom. Their
heightened awareness of the significance of death was
neither morbid nor fatalistic. It awakened in them
great sensitivity, extraordinary gifts of perception and
indomitable courage.

Echoes of this same spirit, born of clear-eyed
contemplation of death, can be traced in almost all
cultures. The tradition stretches from the earliest
known civilizations of Asia through to those of the
first peoples of the Western hemisphere. Today, we
find it taking fresh form in the movement for
conscious dying, for an end to the social taboo on
death and for "green burials".

A mystery so deep

It has been argued that people, particularly in
industrialized nations, have lost touch with death.
Dealing with death has been largely handed over to
the professionals and the funeral industry. This shift
has changed our view of death itself. But it was not
always so.

Four or five generations ago death was very
different. The vast majority of people died at home.
Care of the dying and arrangements for their burial
were intimate family responsibilities. Beyond the
circle of the immediate family, funeral and grief
rituals often involved entire communities. Death was
not a stranger; infant mortality and lower life
expectancy rates meant that the encounter with
death was more frequent and inescapable. "Now,"
says the social historian Philippe Aries, "everything
goes on in town as if no one died any more."

Yet awareness of the presence of death in our
midst formed part of the earliest Christian tradition.
In the great cathedrals of Europe the tombs of the
mighty were adorned with graphic reminders of the
reality of death. In the Middle Ages, the Christian
world had its own 'book of the dead', the *Ars*

What is death?

Death is part of the
unending cycle of nature,
part of the immensity of
creation, rather than a mere
abyss at the end of life.

•

Death is to be understood as
an integral part of existence,
rather than shunned as a
dreaded enemy.

•

Death is a great teacher,
offering striking insights
into life, rather than a
merciless threat to all that
we hold dear.

•

Death is to be faced
consciously, even embraced,
rather than avoided
at all costs.

•

Death is to be discussed and
prepared for openly with
those we love, rather than a
social taboo to be hushed up
or hidden away.

•

Death, and all that surrounds
it, is a precious interval for
both the dying and the
living. It is a mystery that
deserves – and rewards –
profound respect.

Death is not monolithic. Faced with the fact of being mortal, the human spirit has responded with remarkable diversity, vibrant imagination and often with a breathtaking sense of freedom. An Inuit shaman begins the voyage to the beyond carrying the animals and birds that have been the spiritual companions of healing in this life.

Moriendi, the "Art of Dying". Meditation upon death, often with a preserved skull as a memento mori, a "reminder of death", was part of the religious and philosophical tradition.

In a renowned 17th-century English book of death, *The Rules and Exercises of Holy Dying*, the author, Chaplain to King Charles I, insisted that the wise review their lives daily in the light of death, adding "it is a great art to die well and to be learned by men in health".

Those who have reacted against the modern death industry have looked to these historical roots. They have found inspiration there for what has become the Natural Death Movement.

"To civilize death, to bring it home and make it no longer a source of dread, is one of the greatest challenges of the age," is part of the manifesto of The Natural Death Centre, established in London in 1991. "Gradually, dying may come to hold again the place it used to occupy in the midst of life: not a terror but a mystery so deep that man would no more wish to cheat himself of it than to cheat himself of life."

PART ONE

Nature's way

THERAPIES
·
EXERCISES
·
PERSPECTIVES

Winter is on my head, but eternal spring is in my heart. The nearer I approach the end, the plainer I hear around me the immortal symphonies of the worlds which invite me.

VICTOR HUGO

Our deepest needs

In a memorable talk to a group of doctors and other health professionals, a charismatic lecturer asked the assembled experts, "What does a dying person need?"

In silence she wrote down all the suggestions from her audience on the blackboard. Then she changed the word "dying" to "living" and asked if the needs of the dying were different in any way to those of the living. No one proposed any changes.

Then the question was rewritten to read: "What do you need?". In the ensuing silence there was a realization that what each person felt to be their own deepest needs were those they had first said to be the needs of the dying.

One of the greatest mistakes we make is to think that dying people need to be treated in a way that is fundamentally different to the living. Or that their needs and our own needs are different.

Our common humanity is rooted in our deepest needs. These include the profound longing to accept ourselves completely across the full spectrum of living and dying, to be able to extend that complete acceptance to others and to be loved unconditionally in that same way by them.

This book is designed to help you to meet precisely those needs, whether you are a person with a critical illness, caring for a dying person or encountering the reality of death in other ways.

Essential exercises

This first part of the book contains key exercises on pages 42–9. These lay the essential foundations for many of the treatments and practices recommended later. Simple as these initial exercises are, they will prove immensely valuable in helping you find and share personal strength with others.

While I thought I was learning how to live, I have been learning how to die.

LEONARDO DA VINCI

Complementary care

This part of the book also introduces you to various therapies which complement conventional treatment in the care of the dying. An increasing number of support and self-help groups include such therapies in their services or directories, and many hospices offer them.

One reason for this trend is the growing attention being given to the psychological, emotional and spiritual needs of dying people. Complementary therapies help improve quality of life and enhance overall wellbeing, as well as giving symptom relief.

The therapies act as an antidote to stress and anxiety, resulting in better sleep and better tolerance of medical procedures. In particular, because of the unconditional acceptance of the therapist or caregiver, the treatments aid relaxation and ease distress, thus helping patients acknowledge and accept their changing circumstances.

Most complementary therapies have a common underlying approach. They view each person as an individual and aim to treat the whole person and not simply suppress specific symptoms. They seek internal balance and respect natural processes, including ageing and dying.

These health systems respect the impact of the mind's energies on the body, hence the importance placed on relaxation and visualization exercises. They can also ease mental stress through bodywork such as massage and aromatherapy.

When patients turn to complementary therapies, it is often their way of exercising choice and autonomy. The experience may offer them an important vehicle of expressing themselves and coming to terms with their trauma.

Complementary therapies are also beneficial for those caring for the dying. For nurses, it is an opportunity to develop and use skills of touch, caring and intensive one-to-one treatment which may be missing in the normal clinical setting. For carers in the family, using complementary therapies such as massage may be a way of enabling them to do something in an otherwise "hopeless" situation.

Herbs, oils and vibrations

The complementary therapies from which the basic techniques in this book are drawn are deeply rooted in the holistic approach to both life and death. The next four pages give you a very brief overview of each therapy and, in some cases, the fundamental procedure involved in using them. Step-by-step detailed applications are found with the corresponding symptoms described in Part Two: Loving and caring. Manuals on the use of all the therapies are included in the Resources (pages 184–7).

Herbal remedies

Herbal medicine is one of the oldest healing traditions in the world. Although it is best to contact a professional herbalist for diagnosis and treatment, the herbs recommended in this book can be easily obtained and used safely at home. Most herbs contain several active ingredients which work together to ensure that they can be absorbed by the body without adverse side-effects. They can be made into teas, prepared or purchased as tinctures, or added to food and drink.

CAUTION: When properly prepared and used, herbal remedies are gentle, safe and effective. Always follow instructions carefully and never exceed recommended doses.

Bach flower remedies

A system drawing on the energy of plants, flowers and trees was developed early in the 20th century by the eminent British physician, Dr Edward Bach. The tinctures form a complete and simple system that is aimed at the emotional imbalances that can lie at the root of disease and unhappiness. They are entirely safe and can be used by anyone.

Preparing herbal tea
A standard adult dose of herbal tea is made with 1oz (28g) of dried herb to 1 pint (600ml) of water or a teaspoonful per cup. Double the amount if the herb is fresh; halve it or quarter it for children. Place the herbs in a warmed pot, pour on boiling water and cover to prevent the loss of oils into the atmosphere. Leave to infuse for 10 minutes and strain. Drink immediately or store in the refrigerator in an airtight container for up to two days.

Preparing Bach flower tinctures
The two methods of making up a tincture are to dilute two drops into a glass of water to be sipped at intervals; or, for long-term care, to prepare a treatment bottle. Printed instructions are supplied with all the remedies.

Aromatherapy

Aromatic essences are extracted from roots, leaves, flowers or fruits and have been used since antiquity to cleanse and heal both the body and mind. Many pharmacists and health food shops stock aromatherapy oils which can be safely massaged into the skin, used in a bath or inhaled. The use of specific oils is indicated in distinctive charts throughout Part Two.

CAUTION: Essential oils used in aromatherapy can have powerful effects. Never employ high dosages, always follow instructions carefully and be aware of any contraindications.

When using more than one oil at a time, ensure that the *total number of drops* does not exceed the recommended dosage for each application given below.

Using the essential oils
In a bath
Put 6–8 drops in bathwater at a comfortable temperature and swish water well. Soak in the bath for 10 minutes.
Massage
Add 15 drops to 50ml of a carrier oil, such as sweet almond oil or sunflower seed oil, to create the massage oil. For single applications add 2–3 drops to one teaspoon of the carrier oil.

Inhalation
Put 3–4 drops on a paper tissue or in a basin of warm water and inhale for up to 10 minutes twice a day. **Note:** this method should not be used by asthmatics.
Vaporizer
Follow the instructions given by the manufacturer of the vaporizer or "aromatherapy stone".

Colour and sound therapy

Both colour and sound are potent forms of natural energy. Their sensitive vibrations can be used to deal with emotional difficulties and to aid the treatment of related physical symptoms. Guidance is available from specialists, but also published in self-help books. Both colour and sound are worth considering in creating an appropriate environment for a person's inner work at the time of death. Specific suggestions are on pages 94–5.

Bodywork and energy

The therapies presented below include forms of bodywork, exercise and relaxation techniques that have been used with powerful effect on people suffering from a wide range of disorders.

Massage

Therapeutic massage is one of the most powerful forms of healing known to humanity. Fundamental techniques, which may relieve pain (see Part Two), can be learned by carers and used very effectively at home and in hospices and hospitals. Massage also plays an important role in enabling people to deepen the contact they make with each other.

A woman interviewed in one hospital study described the value to her of massage therapy: "I wasn't aware of feeling sad or even sorry for myself, but suddenly tired and weary with the effort of pretending I was OK. The touch was so accepting and compassionate, the image that went through my mind was that of being a child again, comforted by my mother. The massage itself was good – relaxing and so gentle that I began to think of other things. Again I cried at the end when the massage therapist covered me with a towel – it was done so lovingly and caringly. The whole experience made me feel I was worth caring about."

Shiatsu

Shiatsu (pronouced shee-at-soo) is a Japanese word meaning "finger pressure". Treatment consists of still, relaxed pressure at various points on the body. The receiver's internal energy is enhanced and rebalanced. Some very helpful techniques that can be employed at home by carers have been incorporated in the holding and touching techniques for specific conditions given in Part Two.

Energy exercise (Chi Kung)

The oldest medical tradition in the world is to be found in China, where great emphasis is laid on regulating the "life force" or "internal energy" (referred to as "Chi") of the human body. Gentle exercises, including some which are completely stationary, are still used in Chinese hospitals today, often in the treatment of patients with cancer and other serious diseases. They are now being introduced to people in the West and can be learned and practised at home. A basic exercise is described on page 91.

Relaxation techniques

Many of our aches and other complaints are the direct result of stress. Natural health systems promote relaxation, with positive benefits for our joints, muscles, nervous system and internal organs. In addition, there are specific mental and physical exercises that can be learned – at any age and in almost any state of health – to help relieve stress. An essential relaxation exercise can be found on pages 44–5 and other exercises for stress relief are on pages 88–91.

Other health systems

The complementary therapies presented on these pages are only a few of those now available. The fact that other therapies have not been included in this book does not mean that they are inappropriate in the care of dying people. However, the treatments that have been selected give the ordinary reader a range of techniques that can be safely used, without extensive training, in response to some of the most common symptoms experienced by people with illnesses that have progressed beyond cure by conventional medical methods. In this way, the treatments may be of imme-diate use in such cases, and also serve as a basic introduction to the wider world of complementary medicine.

Often people seeking health care that complements conventional medical treat-ment turn to acupuncture and homeo-pathy. Both are best used under the care of professional practitioners. See the Resources (pages 184–7) for information on registers of practitioners.

Common questions

As complementary therapies become better known and more widely available, people have many questions about their safety, their relationship to conventional medicine and how to use them. Some of the most common questions are presented here.

Is there any conflict between these therapies and conventional medical treatments?

These therapies are known as *complementary therapies* because they complement and support conventional medicine. They are not alternatives to it and do not conflict with it. For example, massage and relaxation techniques are being increasingly used in hospitals to supplement the surgical and pharmacological treatment of patients.

Should I consult my doctor before using these therapies?

To give you the best possible care, your doctor should have the fullest possible information about you. If you want to avail yourself of complementary therapies, and particularly if you are on medication and are considering taking herbal treatments, it is best to be frank about this with your doctor.

Can I use these therapies at home, in hospital and in a hospice?

All the therapies in this book can be used in any of these settings. Some hospitals and hospices have staff specially trained in them; in others, you will need to discuss how best to use the techniques in the light of your needs and the available facilities.

Can I use these therapies to cure specific illnesses?

Some complementary systems, such as homeopathy, acupuncture and herbal medicine, have a long-established tradition of curative treatment. If you are seeking possible cures, you should always consult a specialist in a particular therapy. The techniques offered in this book are not cures. They have been selected because experience has shown that they can often help with some common physical and emotional difficulties experienced by dying people and their carers.

For those of us who learn to love life, with all of its changes, death should not be a fearful event. When it is your time to pass, it should be with your mind wide open and your prayer in your heart.

SUN BEAR
OF THE BEAR TRIBE
MEDICINE SOCIETY

What are the risks and side-effects of these therapies?

Compared to certain types of powerful drug, the risks and side-effects associated with the techniques outlined in this book are minimal. However, if you experience any unusual symptoms following their use, you should always consult your doctor.

If I use these therapies on a dying person, will I catch their disease?

In the vast majority of cases this would not be a risk, and then only if you were touching open wounds. If you have any fears about this, consult your doctor.

Do bodywork therapies spread diseases like cancer throughout the person's body?

Doctors who have studied this question report that there is no evidence to support the fear that "massage spreads cancer". If, however, you have any doubts about the appropriateness of massage or other bodywork, seek the advice of your palliative care team or other medical staff.

Where there is no doctor

It is sometimes said that the denial of death has a particularly urban quality. In agricultural communities, death in all its natural forms is so much a part of daily life, that it does not appear to acquire the same morbid terror with which it holds the industrialized world in thrall.

In the mountains of Mexico, the farmers use a health manual to provide primary health care in the absence of medical facilities. The fame of this manual, *Where There Is No Doctor*, has spread throughout Latin America and beyond. Translations and adaptations now exist in numerous countries and languages throughout the world.

Among the 500 pages, crammed with advice on everything from sore gums to cancer, is a single page on death.

Whether you are dying yourself or helping a dying person, you may find great power in its simple words (see overleaf).

Where there is no doctor

"People who have lived fully are not usually afraid to die. Death is, after all, the natural end of life.

We often make the mistake of trying to keep a dying person alive as long as possible, no matter what the cost. Sometimes this adds to the suffering and strain for both the person and their family. There are many occasions when the kindest thing to do is not to hunt for 'better medicine' or a 'better doctor' but to be close to and supporting of the person who is dying. Let them know that you are glad for all the time, the joy and sorrow you have shared, and that you, too, are able to accept their death. In the last hours, love and acceptance will do far more good than medicines.

Old or chronically ill people would often prefer to be at home, in familiar surroundings with those they love, than to be in a hospital. At times, this may mean that the person will die earlier. But this is not necessarily bad. We must be sensitive to the person's feelings and needs, and to our own. Sometimes a person who is dying suffers more knowing that the cost of keeping him or her alive causes the family to go into debt or the children to go hungry. The person may ask simply to be allowed to die – and there are times when this may be the wise decision.

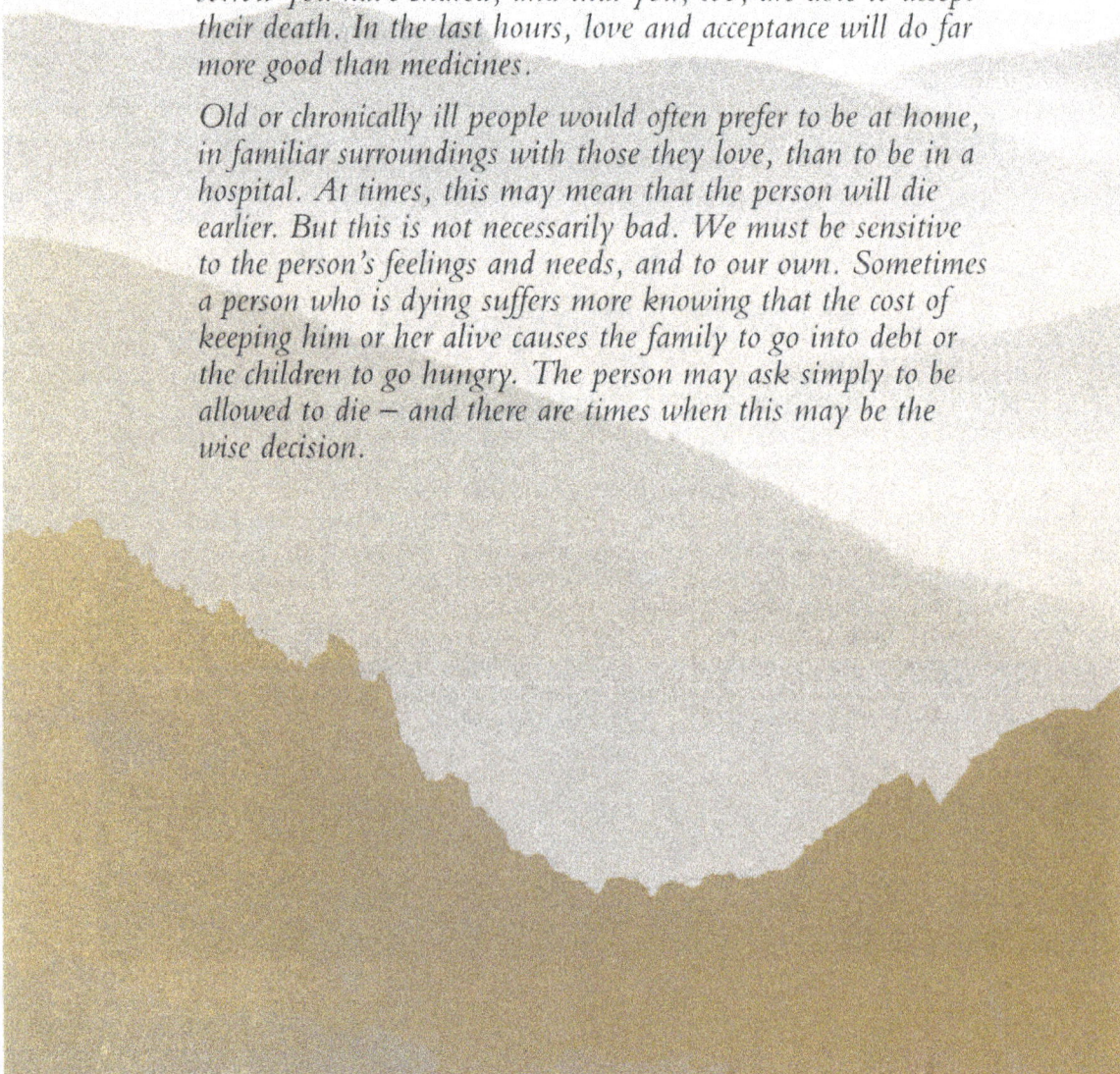

Yet some people fear death. Even if they are suffering, the known world may be hard to leave behind. Every culture has a system of beliefs about death and ideas about forms of life after death. These ideas, beliefs, and traditions may offer some comfort in facing death.

Death may come upon a person suddenly and unexpectedly or may be long-awaited. How to help someone we love accept and prepare for their approaching death is not an easy matter. Often the most we can do is offer support, kindness, and understanding.

Both kindness and honesty are important. Anyone who is dying often knows it, partly by what their own body tells them and partly by the fear or despair they see in those who love them. Whether young or old, if a person who is dying asks for the truth, tell them, but tell them gently. Weep if you must, but let them know that even as you love them, and because you love them, you have the strength to let them leave you. This will give them the strength and courage to accept leaving you. To let a dying person know these things, you need not say them. You need to feel and show them.

We must all die. Perhaps the most important task of the healer is to help people accept death when it can or should no longer be avoided, and to help ease the suffering of those who still live."

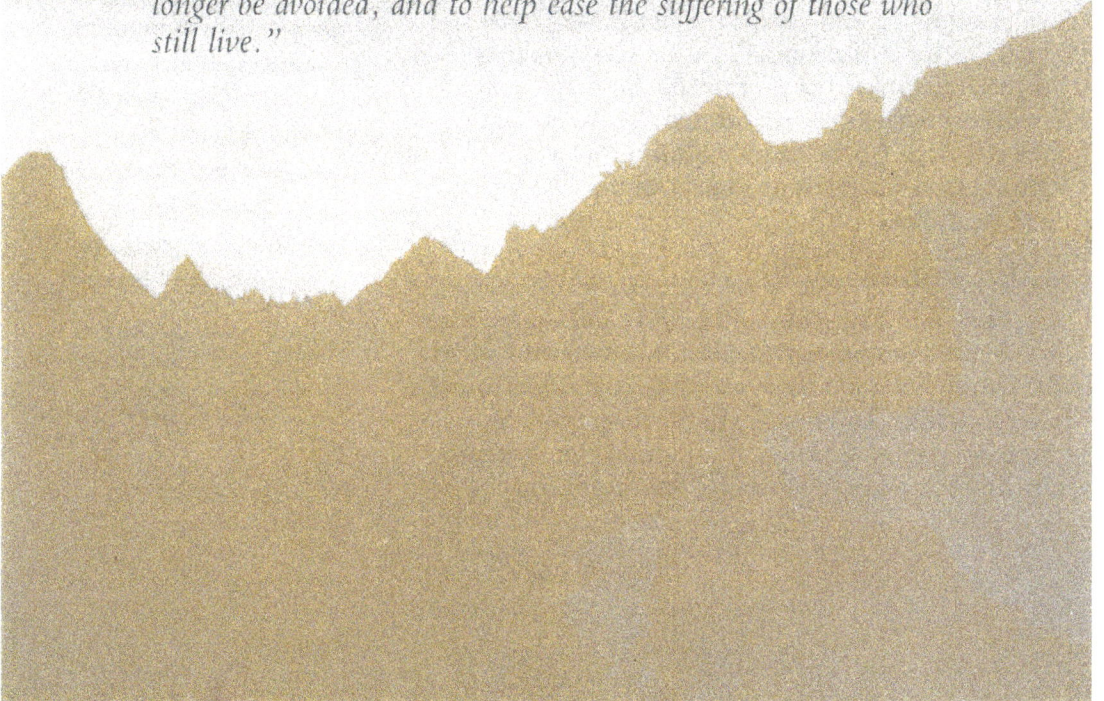

In the mirror of death

Death is the only wise adviser that we have. An immense amount of pettiness is dropped if your death makes a gesture to you, or if you catch a glimpse of it, or if you just have the feeling that your companion is there watching you.

CARLOS CASTANEDA

Mirrors have startling properties. The energy which they reflect back is of a greater intensity than the light which strikes them. We can find ourselves mesmerized by the images we see in them. They show things – and ourselves – in a different light and reveal qualities of which we were unaware, and we sometimes would prefer not to see.

The encounter with death is similar. In the words of a modern-day rabbi, "It is nothing to fear in itself, but it concentrates the mind powerfully in examining what it is we mean by life."

The contemplation of death has been part of the world's spiritual traditions through the ages. More than two and a half millennia ago, early Buddhists placed the reality of death at the heart of their meditative practices. The Athenian philosopher Socrates, imprisoned and sentenced to death in the 5th century BCE for calling into question the complacent assumptions of his society, told his followers "those who rightly love wisdom are practising dying, and death to them is the least terrible thing in the world". In the late medieval Christian tradition, the author of *The Rules and Exercises of Holy Dying* advocated the use of death as a mirror for the "daily examination of our actions" and warned his readers not to wait until they were on their death beds.

In the fullness of life

You may find that many of the ideas and suggestions in this book prompt questions not just about care of the dying, but about how we treat each other in the fullness of life. To remind you of this perspective, there are trigger questions throughout the book in which you are invited to look "in the mirror".

People who have been trained in the contemplation of death find that their lives change.

They tend to be:

more accepting of themselves

more accepting of others

more generous and caring

more joyful in daily life

more aware of the sacred dimension of life

more intensely focused on the present

less selfish

less possessive

less anxious

less obsessive about the past and future

In the words of one: *"I thought I was dying, but I was preparing myself to live."*

The American psychiatrist Elisabeth Kübler-Ross, who is widely credited with pioneering a new attitude towards dying people, saw that those who were prepared to contemplate their own deaths *in advance* reaped unexpected benefits as the rest of their lives unfolded. "If you can face and understand your ultimate death," she wrote, "perhaps you can learn to face and deal productively with each change that presents itself in your life. Through a willingness to risk the unknown, to venture forth into unfamiliar territory, you can understand the search for your own self – the ultimate goal of growth. Through reaching out and committing yourself to dialogue with fellow human beings, you can begin to transcend your individual existence, becoming at one with yourself and others. And through a lifetime of such commitment, you can face your final end with peace and joy, knowing that you have lived your life well."

The tempest

The encounter with death can tear us completely loose from our moorings. One moment we are living normally, as if anchored in a familiar harbour. In the next moment we are at the mercy of tumultuous forces we can neither understand nor control. Our daily routines, our ordinary surroundings and all the people to whom we are attached are utterly transformed. All our assumptions and expectations are wiped out, just as if the central operating program of our computer had been irretrievably destroyed.

Although we may be surrounded by people and professionals who treat death as a physical event involving symptoms and treatments, our fundamental experience of it – whether we are dying ourselves or caring for someone else – is deeply emotional. Whether we express it or not, we are confronted with the full range of our emotional conditioning. Being able to understand and deal with the chaotic fury of those feelings and with the feelings of others lies at the heart of learning to die well.

Caring for each other

Suffering itself, the hard truth of disease, old age, and dying can become, against all odds and expectations, manifestations of a transcendent and always present goodness, a tender, cosmic, benevolence.

FATHER LAURENCE FREEMAN

Caring for a dying person can be stressful, exhausting and relentless. It is an open-ended commitment and can literally extend for years. Carers can break down under the never-ending pressure. Relationships may be stretched to the breaking point.

Carers' lifestyles may be altered beyond recognition. They may be beset with every conceivable worry, from financial to emotional. Some feel helpless in the face of the resentment that wells up in them. Others are obsessed with feelings of incompetence, inadequacy and frustration. To that is added the grief they feel at the impending death and their fear that they may not be able to cope.

Even in the face of these pressures, countless people find caring to be deeply rewarding, full of meaning and purpose, and the ultimate fulfilment of their love for the other person.

Unique quality of care

If you are a carer, you are one of the most important resources available to the dying person. Look after yourself in the best possible way so that you can be of maximum benefit when they most need your unique quality of care.

It is important to remember that your state of being has an effect on the dying person. If you are too anxious and run down, you might communicate a sense of unease to the person you are caring for, no matter how loving you are trying to be.

The relaxation and stress reduction treatments in this book can be used to sustain all the carers as well as the dying person, and thereby increase the quality of care.

Reversing roles

A distinctive feature of many of the exercises and treatments in this book is that in certain instances they can be used or directed by the dying person to sustain and care for the caregivers. Indeed, health professionals often notice that the carer may be experiencing more anxiety than the patient and be in desperate need of attention, reassurance and support.

People with long-term illnesses need considerable care, but there is still much they may be able to contribute – depending on their varying state of health. One thing they can often do is to help their carers relax: giving some simple hand massage, guiding them through stress reduction exercises or reminding them of the relaxation advice that carers need, but all too often overlook.

This sort of mutual support, as long as it is possible, can be extraordinarily rewarding for all involved and transform the experience of dying.

Some carers feel compelled to carry the entire burden of responsibility themselves, yet resent the fact that other family members are not available to help them. This resentment lingers, is often unexpressed and can cause many tensions. Assertiveness training can help, enabling carers to examine and express their needs more effectively, communicate more freely (with less timidity or less aggression) and adapt to the new role they find they must play.

Children's help

It is sometimes wrongly assumed that children in the household are merely an additional burden on the carers. There is even the fear that children may be disturbed by the presence of a dying person in the family. But children can learn and use many of the massage and other techniques in this book; they may discover extremely useful and powerful ways of communicating with and supporting the dying person and the carers. This will depend very much on the circumstances in each family and the emotional openness of all the adults involved.

Cultivating energy

Dying and caring for the dying have certain characteristics in common with long-distance athletic events. You need to sustain and conserve your energy. You need to pace yourself so that you don't burn out in the very early stages. You need considerable stamina and patience. You need firmness of purpose and readiness to face the unexpected. This is all the more true of the encounter with death, since the duration is so unpredictable, the emotional pressure intense and the stretches of boredom, restlessness and pain potentially long and unrelieved.

At some points the people doing the caring may experience greater pressure, distress and difficulty than the person who is dying. The energy levels of both will vary considerably from the outset of the illness right through to the moment of death. So it is important from the very start to undertake some form of appropriate energy cultivation so that you are able to cope with what lies ahead to the best of your ability.

Internal strength

What you need is a form of training that nurtures the body's natural energies, is appropriate for your age and condition, is not punishing and has a powerful, calming effect on your mind and nervous system. Such training is part of the unique contribution of Oriental medicine to world culture. It includes slow, gentle exercise like Tai Chi and Chi Kung, and other related methods of cultivating the body's internal energy such as Yoga. Not surprisingly, such systems are commonly practised by people in their middle years and continued through the last years of their lives.

In the case of those caring for the dying, such energy work can help develop stamina, presence of mind and inner balance, while sustaining physical suppleness. In the case of a person with a terminal condition, it works on two levels. It helps regulate the body's energies and helps harmonize the profound transformation of body and mind.

Death is the great adventure beside which moon landings and space trips pale into insignificance.

JOSEPH BAYLY

Gentle exercise

Gentle exercise can be helpful in promoting wellbeing and revitalizing people who are not capable of strenuous activity. Elderly people are increasingly turning to, and taking classes in, this type of exercise.

Chi Kung literally means "internal energy exercise" and takes many forms. One of the most powerful is known as "Standing Like a Tree", which can be adapted for use in the course of illness (see page 91).

Tai Chi includes fundamental exercises to keep all the joints of the body relaxed and a series of slow, graceful movements that promote inner balance and mental harmony. See Resources (pages 184–7).

Chinese hand balls are now widely available in Oriental craft shops and health centres. They are designed to be rolled in the hand in order to stimulate the acupuncture points which are concentrated in the fingers and connect to all major internal organs. Regular practice keeps the mind alert.

IN THE MIRROR

These tried and tested methods of sustaining your energy and adapting to the pressures of life are not only valuable for people who are dying or working with the dying. They have proved useful as a way of bringing health and harmony into people's lives at any stage, particularly if their lifestyle includes coping with daily stress. If you develop a solid background of some form of preventative health care like this, you are all the better equipped to deal with extreme crises when they arise.

Even if you do not feel it is appropriate – or possible – for you to undertake the types of exercise recommended above, it is still important to ask yourself:

Is there any other way in which you can regularly take exercise and care for your own health at this point in your life?

Are you making sure that this is true also for the rest of your family and others you love?

The loving presence

I want to assure you that it is a blessing to sit at the bedside of a dying patient. Dying doesn't have to be a sad and horrible matter. Instead, you can experience many wonderful and loving things. What you learn from dying you can pass on to your children and your neighbours, and maybe our world would become a paradise again. I believe now is the time to start.

ELISABETH KÜBLER-ROSS

Like everything that lives, each of us is a field of energy. The more sensitive we are, the more we can feel the immediate effect that other people's energy has on us. This is particularly true of people who are ill and those who are dying.

Most dying people are particularly sensitive to the authentic presence of someone who is fully attentive to them. As a carer, making yourself available to the dying person in this way does not require special expertise or knowing "what to say". It is, quite literally, the interaction of two energy fields. It requires simply being there, fully present with complete acceptance, regardless of what is happening.

Being relaxed

Your presence begins with the way you relate to yourself. So while you begin with the desire to be helpful to the other person, in reality you have to begin with assessing yourself.

Normally, the energy pattern we project outwards in times of stress is disturbing to others, but we are often unaware of it ourselves. There are tell-tale signs: tense neck and shoulder muscles, pressure in the chest area or head, frequent blinking and rapid eye movements. This is usually because our energy constantly rushes upwards when we are under stress, causing tension, headaches and restlessness.

The exercises on the next pages will help you relax and these can be extremely useful at various times. Although they appear simple, they affect and can transform your entire energy field.

You can do them before working with the dying person, while sitting beside them or while watching them sleep. Your relaxed presence will also have a healing effect on everyone else around you.

In calm waters

If you are called upon to care for a dying person you can become exhausted and frustrated. Not only has your normal life been disrupted, but there is little to show for the endless drudgery of caring. Dismay, resentment, anger and helplessness are inevitable. You may find yourself wishing it were "all over", only to be overwhelmed by guilt and sadness at having, in a sense, wished that your loved one were dead.

Even in the midst of this rollercoaster of the emotions, death is a great teacher. It is as if you were sitting in a small boat in waters which have been becalmed. There is no wind to fill your small sail and you are too far out to sea to be able to take up the oars and reach land. You have only one companion in your tiny vessel and that person is dying. You have always loved them and even now you would do anything you could for them. But the little boat quickly teaches you that frantic efforts create unwelcome disturbance. To the dying person it might almost seem as if you are thrashing around in a desperate effort to get out of the boat, save your own life and abandon them. What they need instead is for you to abide quietly with them in those calm waters. You are both still alive, and both dying, but at different rates. In the stillness of the little boat, you enter into the significance of being mortal.

The body of wisdom

Your body is a body of wisdom. It lies at the basis of your sense of being alive and enables you to know what is happening both to you and around you. This wisdom continues to be available to you throughout the process of dying.

In many spiritual traditions great emphasis is laid on giving up the body at the time of death, but that cannot be done by neglecting or abusing the body. It must be loved and listened to.

Unfortunately, many of us become disconnected from our bodies as a result of the culture in which we live and so, in a very real sense, we are never fully present. Being present lies at the heart of dying well, both for the dying person and for anyone who wishes to support them.

Grounding yourself

The exercise on the facing page is designed to rekindle your awareness of your body and hence, the ground of your being. It makes use of the power of your central nervous system and the energy pathways associated with your spine. You rebalance the flow of your internal energy, lower your centre of gravity and make your nervous system more stable. You connect with the strength and nurturing energy of the earth beneath you. This ability to ground yourself empowers any other practice associated with dying or helping the dying.

If you are a carer, you may yourself be under a great deal of stress. Your energy may be depleted or unsettled. Before you massage or attempt any hands-on therapy, therefore, you need to balance your own energy using this exercise. Otherwise you will simply be passing on your anxiety to the dying person. You can practise it on your own or use the instructions to guide the dying person or another carer.

I'm gettin' ready to go. How am I doin' it? I'm layin' aside every weight and sin that does so easily beset me and I'm gettin' light for the flight.

WILLIE MAY
FORD SMITH

Balancing your energy

1. Sit comfortably, trying if possible to keep your back straight. Rest your feet flat on the floor.

2. Close your eyes or lower your gaze.

3. Relax your shoulders and chest, and breathe naturally.

4. Bring your mind to bear on the fact that you are sitting. Try to feel the weight of your entire upper body resting on your sitting bones and the bones themselves feeling the pressure of that weight.

5. Focus your awareness on the bottom of your spine. Try to feel the strength of the base of your spine as it supports the full weight of your spinal cord and skull.

6. As you become more aware of the sense of strength at the base of your spine, allow your neck, shoulders and chest to relax further, as if they were allowing the spine to bear their weight fully.

7. Then, without losing that feeling, let your mind also be aware of the very top of your head. Imagine your head being very gently supported, as if suspended from above by a fine cord.

8. Then let your attention move slowly down from the top of your head, down your neck and slowly down your backbone. Imagine each of the vertebrae in your neck and back, and as you call each one to mind, imagine it is relaxing and becoming warm. It is almost as if a warm current were starting to travel from the top of your spine slowly down to the very bottom.

Repeat the eight steps of the exercise at least three times, pausing at the end each time to experience the relaxation of the muscles in the upper body and the sense of weight and strength at the base of the spine.

To conclude, simply transfer your attention to the rising and falling of your breath. Rest calmly for a minute before ending the exercise.

If you have trouble imagining the vertebrae in your spine, imagine your whole back is covered in thick, caked mud. Imagine you are under a warm shower and "feel" the rushing water loosen the mud and gradually wash it away, so that the softened mud and warm water run slowly down your back, until your entire back is cleansed and warmed.

If you cannot sit up straight, and if it causes you no pain or discomfort, try propping yourself up as far as possible in bed. Otherwise, try the exercise lying as straight as possible in bed, adapting it to allow you to concentrate your attention.

Progressive relaxation

Relaxation is an essential element in all the practices associated with caring for the dying and also in preparing oneself for death. Progressive relaxation is a highly successful technique that relies simply on tensing and then relaxing the major muscle groups throughout the body. It can be done in any position, although it is probably easiest lying flat on your back with pillows for comfort. If you have trouble sleeping, this exercise can be a great help.

The full instructions are given below. You can follow them silently or ask someone to read them to you. Working together through the sequences can be extremely helpful for both people and ensures a smooth, slow pace. The timings are shown in the first sequence. Follow this model throughout.

Adapting the
relaxation method
Some people may not be able to cope with all the tensing and holding, or be able to hold their breath for as long as 5 seconds. They may find 12 sequences too many. In that case, reduce the time and select only those sequences that are easiest. If tensing the muscles is too demanding, try the visualization of light recommended on pages 150–1.

1

1. Keep your legs flat and angle your toes up towards your knees as far as they will go. As you do this breathe in (**5 seconds**). Then relax as you breathe out (**5 seconds**).
2. Again, toes up towards the knees and breathe in (**5 seconds**). Then relax and breathe out (**5 seconds**).
3. Again, pull your toes up towards you and breathe in (**5 seconds**). Then breathe out and relax (**5 seconds**).
   Now, breathe naturally (**10 seconds**).

2

1. Now breathe in and press your toes away from you, as if you were were standing on your toes like a ballet dancer. Hold. Then relax as you breathe out.
2. Again, toes away from you and breathe in. Hold. Then relax and breathe out.
3. Again, press your toes away as far as they will go and breathe in. Hold. Then breathe out and relax. Now, breathe naturally.

3

1. Now breathe in and try to press the backs of your knees down into the bed. Hold. Then relax as you breathe out.
2. Again, knees down into the bed and breathe in. Hold. Relax, breathe out.
3. Again, press your knees down as far as they will go and breathe in. Hold. Breathe out, relax. Breathe naturally.

4

1. Now breathe in and try to press your buttocks down into the bed. Hold. Relax as you breathe out.
2. Again, buttocks down into the bed and breathe in. Hold. Relax and breathe out.
3. Again, press your buttocks down as far as they will go and breathe in. Hold. Breathe, and relax. Breathe naturally.

5

1. Now this time, press the small of your back down into the mattress as you breathe in. Hold. Relax and breathe out.
2. Again, small of the back down and breathe in. Hold. Relax and breathe out.
3. One more time, breathe in. Hold. Breathe out, relax. Breathe naturally.

1, 2

11 12

6 10

5

3 4

7, 8, 9

1. Now as you breathe out stretch your fingers apart as wide as possible. Hold it. Relax, breathe out.
2. Again, wide open, breathe in and hold. Relax, breathe out.
3. Again, stretch, breathe in. Hold. Relax, breathe out. Breathe naturally.

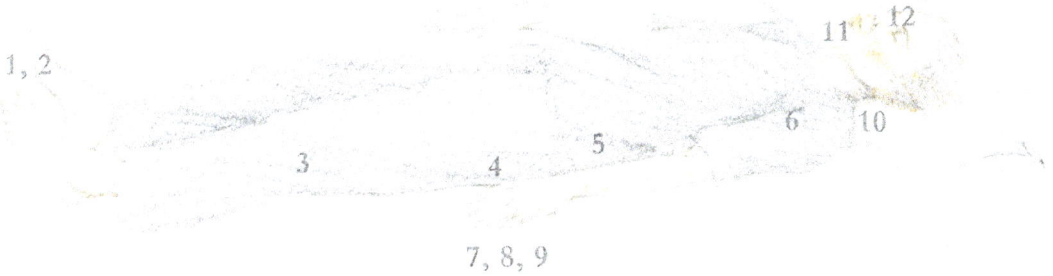

1. Now, your shoulder blades and upper back. Press down into the bed and breathe in. Hold. Relax, breathe out.
2. Again, press down into the mattress with your upper back and breathe in. Hold. Relax, breathe out.
3. One more time as you breathe in. Hold. Breathe out, relax. Breathe naturally.

1. Now, your neck. Press the back of your head firmly down into the bed and breathe in. Hold. Relax, breathe out.
2. Again, press down and breathe in. Hold. Relax, breathe out.
3. One more time as you breathe in. Hold. Breathe out, relax. Breathe naturally.

1. Now make fists with both your hands. Turn them so that the sides of your fists are flat against the bed. Press down with your fists as if you were trying to push yourself up and breathe in. Hold. Relax, breathe out.
2. Again, press down into the mattress with your fists and breathe in. Hold. Relax, breathe out.
3. One more time, press down with your fists and breathe in. Hold. Breathe out, relax. Breathe naturally.

1. Now, try to tuck your chin into your chest as you breathe in. Hold. Relax and breathe out.
2. Again, tuck and breathe in. Hold. Relax, breathe out.
3. One more time. Hold. Relax. Breathe naturally.

1. Now clench both of your fists as tightly as you can as you breathe in. Hold. Relax, breathe out.
2. Again, clench and breathe in. Hold. Relax, breathe out.
3. One more time, clench, breathe in. Hold. Breathe out, relax. Breathe naturally.

1. Finally, to release all the tension stored in your face muscles, try to tighten all the muscles – your forehead, your eyes, your cheeks, your mouth. So, as you breathe in, squeeze up your face. Hold it. Then relax, breathe out.
2. Again, breathe in and squeeze. Hold. Relax, breathe out.
3. Last time, really squeeze every one of those muscles. Hold them. Then relax, breathe out. Now just spend a few minutes being still. Breathe naturally.

The fundamental rhythm

To let go is to lose your foothold temporarily.
Not to let go is to lose your foothold forever.

KIERKEGAARD

One of the greatest difficulties we have is our inability to let go. This is probably the most widespread imbalance we experience in our lives and in our society. You can see it every day, as we consume more and more, drive ourselves harder and harder and experience ever greater levels of tension and anxiety.

Death, the great teacher, is constantly confronting us with this fact. Our fear and our anger, our denial and our revulsion at death often have their roots in our overwhelming urge to "hold on" without the countervailing balance of the energies associated with "letting go". Preparing for death, helping the dying and learning this lesson while we are in the fullness of life are all bound up with cultivating the power of letting go. It is this power which gives rise to compassion, generosity and warmth of spirit.

Letting go

The opening and closing exercise on the facing page is designed to help strengthen your ability to let go. It uses the power of visualization to re-invigorate one of the most fundamental rhythms of our existence.

We are constantly opening and closing, holding on and letting go. As our diaphragm tenses and relaxes, we breathe in and breathe out. As the muscles of our heart contract and relax, blood pulses throughout the body. All our vital functions have this wave-like quality. We eat and we excrete. We wake and we sleep. We remember and we forget. We are attracted to some things, and reject others. The speed of the rhythm varies, but the pattern itself is the thumbprint of our being.

If that pattern is disrupted, our fundamental inner harmony is disturbed, giving rise to emotional difficulties, physical malfunctions and disease. Therefore, under the stress often associated with dying, it can be very helpful to support and sustain this rhythm as fully as possible.

Closed and open

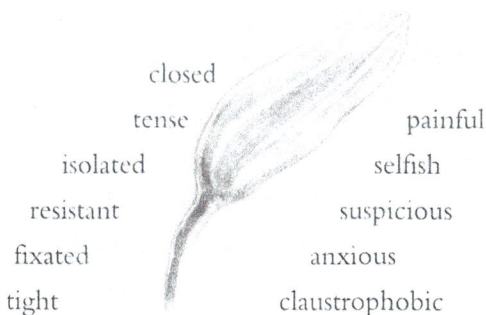

closed
tense   painful
isolated   selfish
resistant   suspicious
fixated   anxious
tight   claustrophobic

The flower is still enclosed in the self-protective bud. It is not yet mature and cannot blossom. It is full of potential, but the energy and pain of holding on are waiting to be transformed.

When the closed bud opens, it is able to blossom. The flower has let go of its early capsule and is ready to release its pollen to the wind or passing creatures. Its true nature is to open wide.

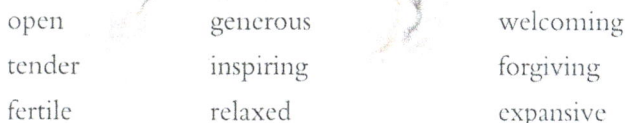

spacious
open   generous   welcoming
tender   inspiring   forgiving
fertile   relaxed   expansive

Opening your heart

You can work with this image at any stage. Imagine that the very centre of the bud is in your heart. Imagine it fully closed. Then allow it to open wide in your mind's eye. Try to use the power of all your senses: see its colour, smell its fragrance, feel its delicacy, hear sounds of nature around it, imagine the sweetness of its extracts. Then watch and feel it close up. Then let it open wide again, imagining that your whole body becomes the open blossom. Repeat this rhythmic visualization for as long as you wish.

You can combine this with the practice of 'taking and sending' (see pages 146–7). When you breathe in, imagine the flower closing down into your heart. When you breathe out, let the flower expand so that the tips of its petals expand to the limits of your body.

The learning curve

If you are dealing with a tremendous, and almost unbearable, whirlpool of emotion, you may feel you are being sucked under by its force. It is important to recognize that the reactions you are now experiencing are not fundamentally different to the emotions with which you have lived all your life. You may be dealing with completely new and shocking events and the intensity of your feelings may be traumatic, but you are not contending with a completely new set of emotions.

In fact, we have been learning about death all our lives. In the words of one philosopher, "our first experience of loss is birth". We also have a lifetime's experience of developing our own strategies and skills for dealing with loss, uncertainty and pain. Sadly, we often forget this heritage of experience when we are told we have a critical medical condition. We feel at a complete loss, as if we had nothing to draw on.

One way of reconnecting with our inner resources is to draw a learning curve of all the important encounters we have had with death – or other major crises, like divorce, job loss, broken hearts and so on – and to identify what we learned from these that we can draw on in the hour of our present need.

3. **Rejected** by first "love of my life". Learn coping strategy: go for long walks. Lesson: don't expect wound ever to heal…

4. **Mid-thirties:** Mother's death. Sometimes seems like low point, sometimes like inspiring example of a person being open, honest and generous in the face of death. I learn how valuable silence by the bedside can be…

1. **Early childhood:** No recollection of fear of death. Intrigued by motorcyclist killed in road accident outside home. Grandfather and two grandmothers die. I want to attend funeral, but not allowed to. Miss important learning opportunity…

2. **Adolescence:** Father dies suddenly. Miss opportunity to see body in morgue, but learn a lot about how to respect the impermanence of everyone's existence…

The value of reminiscence

The inner knowledge of your own emotions, how they express themselves, what strength they give you and what dangers they hold for you can be unlocked in various ways. It can be very helpful to reminisce about the most difficult times in your past, even in your very earliest childhood. You could use a family photo album to help. Many people find that an experience comes to mind, perhaps long forgotten, when they felt they faced uncompromising pain and hopelessness. And yet, encoded in that suffering and what has happened since, they find an inner message, unique to them, which reframes their present crisis in a changed perspective.

8. **Late forties:** Friend's father dies; friend's daughter killed – many precious lessons learned; acceptance. Close colleague may have fatal illness: am I ready for death at any time myself?

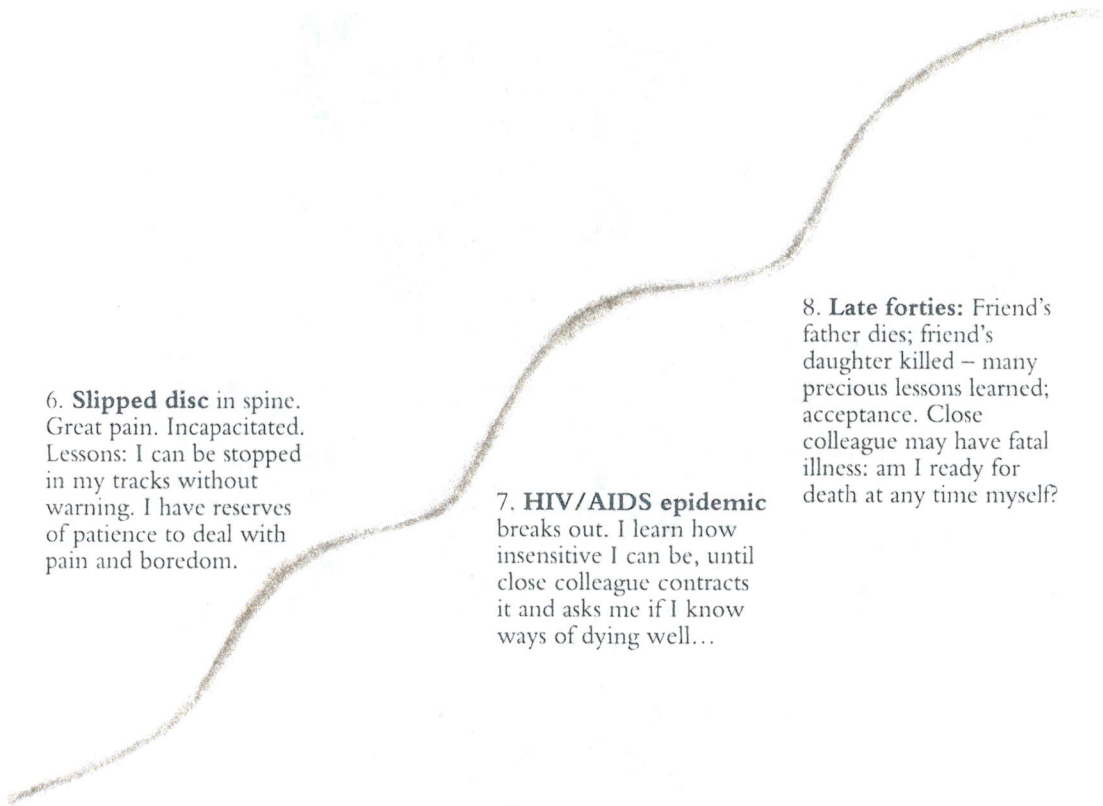

6. **Slipped disc** in spine. Great pain. Incapacitated. Lessons: I can be stopped in my tracks without warning. I have reserves of patience to deal with pain and boredom.

7. **HIV/AIDS epidemic** breaks out. I learn how insensitive I can be, until close colleague contracts it and asks me if I know ways of dying well…

5. **Dear friend killed** in road accident. Lessons: why fear crying? Death can strengthen bonds between people…

The pyramid of support

These learning curve and reminiscence exercises reflect the importance of what is sometimes called the pyramid of support. At its base, and where we find our most authentic and useful support, is our own experience. That is where we need to begin. Then there are other levels of support which may be helpful in various ways.

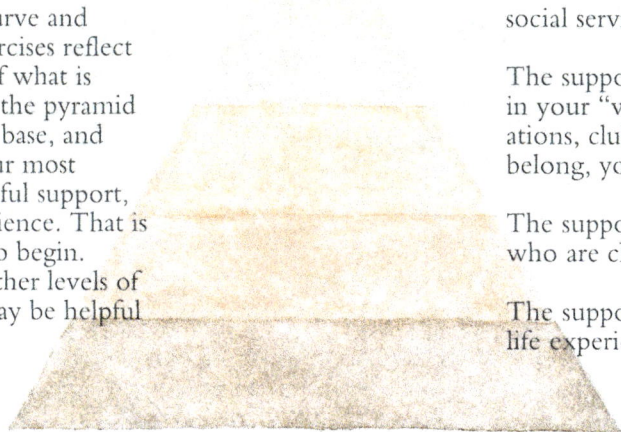

The support of professionals in counselling, medicine and social services…

The support of other people in your "world": the associations, clubs to which you belong, your workplace…

The support of those people who are closest to you…

The support of your own life experience and insight…

PART TWO

Loving and caring

ENVIRONMENTS
·
TREATMENTS
·
BASIC SKILLS

The call of death is a call of love.
Death can be sweet if we answer it in the affirmative,
if we accept it as one of the great eternal forms
of life and transformation.

HERMANN HESSE

The spectrum of care

Few other experiences have the potential to be so tender, so direct and so intense as the time devoted to caring for a dying person. It makes demands that are exhausting and it evokes emotions that are overwhelming. It is subject to no timescale and no predictable boundaries. It can proceed only from one uncertain moment to the next.

Relatives commonly ask that "everything possible" be done for their loved ones. The clinical specialists can now provide a range of medical and other procedures. But it takes love, patience and the support of an open heart to do "everything possible" for a person on the threshold of death's transformation.

Fortunately, the horizon of possibilities now available both before and during protracted illness is expanding. The full spectrum of care extends far beyond medical treatment and affects the entire experience of the person who is facing death. Enlightened medical practice now includes palliative care, which gives great importance to pain relief. The World Health Organization defines palliative care as the active, total care of patients whose disease no longer responds to curative treatment, and for whom the goal must be the best quality of life for them and their families.

Pain and suffering are not automatic, nor are they consistent. They are subject to considerable variation, depending on many factors. One central element is the precise nature of the suffering and the response of the body and nervous system to it. But people's other responses can be affected by many elements:

Are they being cared for at home, in a hospital, a hospice, a nursing home? What freedom do they have to choose that setting?

What information are they getting about their condition? How open and satisfactory is communication with their carers?

What emotional burdens are they carrying?

There is no death, only a change of worlds.

DUWAMISH
INDIAN SAYING

What therapies are being used to deal with the cycle of anxiety, tension and pain?

What support is being given to the person's mental and emotional energies while those of the body are dissipating?

Decisions and resources

If you need care or find yourself having to care for a dying person, you will need to take a number of decisions. These vary from individual to individual and range from decisions on places of care to options for treatment. We are haunted by the spectre of lying helplessly in unbearable pain, unable to move or help ourselves, utterly dependant on overworked doctors and nurses, a burden to ourselves and perhaps all the more so to our partner and children. Our distress may be even greater at the prospect of having this fate befall the people we love most and becoming helpless bystanders as they suffer.

This distress makes many people close up, turn inward and take all burdens stoically upon themselves. But if you want to give the very best care, it is important to remember that caring works best when it is done by a team, whether it is a team of relatives or a mixture of professional carers and friends, backed up by services in your community. So the best advice is to investigate all options fully and be as direct as possible in seeking information and advice from others.

IN THE MIRROR

Since time spent caring for the dying – and accepting such care – can be so rewarding, why is it that people so often fail to take full advantage of it? Even more to the point, why wait until we have little time left to live? You could ask yourself:

If I had only a brief time to live, how would I wish to be cared for and by whom?

If someone I love were facing the same situation, what would I want to do for them? What would I want to express to them?

Am I living and expressing myself in those ways now? Am I already treating the time I spend with others as "precious moments"?

Death trajectories

Unless someone dies unexpectedly in their sleep, has a fatal heart attack or is killed in an incident, death takes time. When a person is diagnosed as having a terminal illness, for example, most people involved with the death start to make predictions about when the person will die. These may be explicit: the doctor says the person has three months to live. Or they may be very subtle: plans for next year's holiday are no longer discussed.

The professionals involved make other assumptions as well. These are often known as "trajectories of dying". It is one way of introducing short-term certainty into a fundamentally uncertain situation. For example, the person may be well enough to be cared for at home in the foreseeable future. When the illness requires more intensive palliative treatment, the structure of care may require regular visits by the health team. Further decisions will need to be made about hospitalization or hospice care and so on. All such decisions need to be regularly reviewed in light of what is actually happening to the person.

How can a sensitive and alive person ever feel secure? We can never be certain of the outcome of our best efforts. The psychic task which a person can and must set for themselves, is not to feel secure, but to be able to tolerate insecurity.

ERIC FROMM

Trajectories

instant death:
heart attack, car crash

Long-term illness:
cancer

Short-term crisis,
followed by
long-term
condition: stroke

Remission

Short-term reprieve

Transitions

The course of an illness is unpredictable. But there are certain transitions that normally occur in the care of a dying person. These vary in duration: some phases may be drawn out and others may be abrupt.

- The person is diagnosed as terminally ill
- Preparations are made for medical treatment and other care
- Only palliative and spiritual care continue
- The person's energies clearly begin to dissipate
- The carers assist at the time of death
- The person is declared clinically dead

Hazard warning

Each person's death is unique to them. At the same time, it is a stranger, both to the person who is ill and to those caring for them. Predictions may be wildly inaccurate. Some people outlive their expected deaths by years, others die far sooner than expected. The person's emotional reaction to their illness may have at least as dramatic effect on the outcome as any medication or other treatment. The human atmosphere created around them also has an unquestionable impact. Conventionally, the assumption is that it is better for a person to live as long as possible, but this too will vary from person to person, depending on the many factors that make their death unique to them.

Relatives and carers may suffer acute inner anguish because of the uncertainty about the course of the illness. Their normal lives are disrupted, creating conflicting pressures of both a practical and an emotional nature. They may have to endure sheer exhaustion and exasperation at the seemingly endless time that dying can take; they are then lacerated with guilt because of those feelings.

The exercises and treatments recommended throughout this book can be of sustained help in supporting everyone involved through the unpredictability and anxiety at all stages of the death process.

Places of care

Where we expect to die has a profound effect on our attitude towards death. At the beginning of this century most people died at home. Today, in many traditional and largely rural societies this remains the case – for the overwhelming proportion of people living on the planet. Thus, it is true to say that most people still die at home, tended by their families and supported by their communities.

However, in heavily industrialized nations the pattern has changed dramatically in the 20th century. Fewer than a quarter of all deaths now take place at home. Nearly sixty per cent of all deaths occur in a hospital; in urban areas it can be seventy per cent, or even higher. The remaining deaths are in hospices, nursing homes for the elderly or similar institutions.

The changing pattern

There are several reasons for this changing pattern. Most obvious is the fact that the provision of medical care has grown and technology is available in hospitals which can save lives in ways that were previously unheard of.

However, several recent studies have shown that although hospital deaths are increasing, the majority of people surveyed do not actually want to die in an institution. Their clear preference is to die at home.

But their wishes often cannot be met. As the proportion of the population that is elderly increases, more and more of them end up either on their own or with only their ageing husbands, wives or partners. The strain faced by these relatives and carers is often decisive in admitting a terminally ill person to hospital, although there is encouraging evidence that older people can be effective carers at home for long periods if supported by a hospice team.

What is appropriate in each case may change over time. Depending on the nature of the illness, a person may spend months being cared for at home, some time in an active treatment hospital and may also be cared for in a hospice, or by a team from a hospice or hospital that provides specialist support.

A Good Death does honour to a whole life.

PETRARCH

The hospice movement

Hospice care for the dying may be provided in purpose-built institutions or by professional teams working in the community with people dying at home. It offers a holistic approach to pain relief, social and family relations and the acceptance of the fact of death. Hospices date back to early Christian "works of mercy"; their modern revival was sparked by British doctor, Dame Cicely Saunders.

Different settings, different experiences

There are a number of questions to consider when thinking about the different places where people receive care. Based on your own experience of what has happened to others in similar situations, you can use the questions to help with decision-making.

Your evaluation of these different settings will depend almost entirely on your own view of what death is and what you believe the experience of dying should be like. It may also be influenced by your lifestyle and by any experience you have already had of hospitals, hospices or nursing homes. Although most people tend to express a preference for dying in their own home, the *nature* of your relations with your family, partner or others will greatly influence that experience – and your decision. Your attitudes may change as your circumstances and options change.

In a hospital, hospice, nursing home or your own home:

Who is there?

What ages? What social mix? What medical conditions do they have? Would you need help adapting to that environment?

Who is in charge?

Do you prefer a hierarchical authority structure or do you need a setting where authority is distributed among everyone involved? How important is it to you to be in charge yourself – and of what aspects of your life?

What is the environment like?

Do you need a supportive environment which conforms to your particular lifestyle? Is this an important issue for you at this point in your life? Would you need help adapting to an institution?

What are you told about your condition?

Information disclosure varies among institutions, but sometimes seems insufficient to the patient and family. How essential to you is full disclosure and discussion? Do your relatives support your views?

What are your decision-making rights?

Who makes the final decisions on your treatment? How important is your own role in decision-making?

How are relatives and carers treated?

Is this important to you? If so, will your relatives and carers be welcomed by everyone involved as part of "your team"?

Dying at home

We have a natural urge to die at home, if we can be looked after properly, because that is where many of us feel most secure and comfortable. Just as more and more people are looking into the possibility of giving birth in their homes, so, too, more and more are choosing – if possible – to continue living at home right up to the moment of death.

We can spend our last days or months in familiar surroundings and in our own private world of people and possessions. If we still have the rest of our family with us, the opportunity to care and be cared for is one of the most precious gifts we can give each other.

Many people's decision about whether to spend their last days at home or whether to bring a dying person home will be determined by very practical considerations. With relatively small or dispersed families, there may be no one in the family physically capable of giving the dying person the sort of attention they need at home. In that case, the focus of caring will need to be located in either a hospital, hospice or residential home – or a combination of all these.

The decision to remain at home raises several major questions. How can we ensure that home care is adequate for the person who is dying? How can we prevent that person's needs becoming an unbearable burden for their partner, the rest of the family or other carers? What are the special skills, equipment or training that will be needed to make it wise for the person to stay at home?

If you are thinking about caring for someone at home or requesting home care for yourself, this part of the book will give you basic advice on arranging the home to meet common needs, learning the fundamental skills of caring and various complementary therapies to improve the quality of life for the person for whom you are caring.

People fear death only because they fail to see that life and death are not separate states but merely two stages of one natural process – that both are present in any given moment.

CHUANG-TZU

Your resources

If you are considering caring for a dying person at home, think carefully about whether you can really offer the kind of support that you would like to. If it proves to be beyond your capacity, it is better to know from the beginning than to start out on an emotional impulse, only to find you cannot provide what the person needs.

To examine your own resources, you could ask yourself:

What are your existing responsibilities – are you fully employed at work in the days? Are you looking after other dependants?

Will you be able to find time or make time to meet your other commitments and also care for the dying person?

If you feel very deeply that you want to care for the dying person at home, are there other arrangements you can make to meet the other responsibilities you have – taking leave from work, arranging for other people to help care for other members of your family?

The best care is done by teamwork. This ensures that everyone's skills can be put to the best use, that there is mutual support during stressful periods and that carers remain fresh and able to help the dying person. Who could you call on to make up such a team? Can you afford professional help? Do you know who to contact for advice?

You need to think carefully about your emotional resources as well. Caring for a dying person can include dealing with problems that some people find distasteful or extremely stressful. For example, how would you cope with giving the person a bed bath or helping them use a bed pan? Would you need assistance in coping with vomiting, incontinence and diarrhoea?

Increasingly, hospices, community-based services and self-help groups are offering support, practical advice and home care to enable dying people to spend as much time at home as possible – and to relieve burdens on their carers. They will also help the whole family assess the various options for care and facilitate the necessary decision-making.

Arranging your home

Home care may begin soon after diagnosis of an illness or it may take place when the person comes home after a period of examination or treatment in hospital. Even if they do not spend all their time at home, some changes will probably be needed.

You will need to discuss which is the most appropriate room for the dying person to use. There are several considerations:

Do you have any choice – you may have only one room – and which considerations are most important, the practical or the emotional?

Is one room more convenient than the others; for example, is it closer to the toilet or more suitable for visitors? Which room is the person's favourite?

Perhaps the bedroom would be best; or perhaps it would be better to reorganize things completely and set aside a room especially arranged in accordance with their wishes.

Living in bed

Often, when we think of caring for a sick person at home, we fall back on an image of a sick-room. The person is alone, bedbound, surrounded by bottles of pills in a room smelling faintly of medication or air freshener. The decision to spend as much as possible of one's remaining time at home can be an opportunity to pay attention to inner needs – what would the person really like to have around them and see in front of them?

Be prepared to make changes as the days and weeks go by. They may wish to continue sharing a room with their partner or spouse. At times, however, this may simply become unrealistic and a burden on both. Sometimes they may wish to be visited and to live in the middle of household life – literally in the "living room". At other times, they may prefer more silence and seclusion.

If the person is largely confined to bed, arrange the bed so that you can have access to it on both sides. This makes it much easier to move or lift the person and to change the sheets. You may also need a hoist or other lifting aids.

A major problem for people who spend long periods in bed is the risk of pressure sores. You can get advice on this from the hospital, prior to bringing

the person home or from your doctor or visiting health worker. In some cases, you will be advised to provide a hospital bed at home and a special pressure-sore mattress (see pages 62–3).

You will need a moveable table on one side or the other, preferably fairly large so that various items can be left on it without getting knocked off. Sometimes, people have a tendency to make the bedside table into a sort of pharmacist's display with all the medications in full view. This creates the distinctive atmosphere of a sick bay. Try to find a way to conveniently arrange medicines and other items away from, but within easy reach of, the person. Then you can concentrate on surrounding them with things that give emotional and mental support, such as books, pictures and writing or drawing materials.

Would the person like to have the opportunity to listen to music or the radio or watch television whenever they wish? How can you arrange that? In some homes, the TV and sound systems are easily portable. If not, the whole family will have to decide how best to share access to them, remembering that the carers and children also need time to relax and be entertained.

Basic skills

There are basic skills that you will need to learn if you are caring for a dying person at home. These are similar to those needed to look after someone who is ill. It is important to spend some time making a personal inventory of what will need to be done, what materials will be needed and what new skills you may need to learn.

It is also important to remember that you do not have to do everything yourself. There may be other sources of help on which you can call, although these will vary depending on your circumstances. Family members and close friends may be happy and willing to take on certain regular responsibilities, such as collecting and doing the laundry, as a way of supporting the dying person and the immediate carers. Or you may be able to call on the services of professionals, such as home helps and hairdressers. Normally, the palliative care team or social services staff will be able to advise you on the community facilities to which you are entitled. For books and organizations that can give you detailed advice on home caring, see the Resources on pages 184–7.

Bedwork

As the person spends more and more time in bed, it is essential that the bed and the area around it be an environment in which they feel relaxed. It is possible to rent medical beds from hospital suppliers. These can be easily raised or lowered, the back can be brought forward or laid flat, and side bars can be used to prevent the person falling. However, the person may have a deep-seated desire to die in their own bed and you should give primacy to their wishes. In that case, castors could be fitted to make the bed easily moveable.

It is important to make the person comfortable and prevent bedsores. There are now special mattresses, known as "eggcrate", which are designed to reduce the likelihood of bedsores developing. Another type of mattress uses pumped air to gently change the contours of contact. You should ask the palliative care team for advice.

A common problem is bedsores developing on the heels (which may press into the bed for hours on end). Special protective footwear is now available.

Artificial "sheepskins" are frequently used under the shoulders, back and buttocks. It is wise to have two in case one is soiled. You can also use foam wedges to change position, if needed, or to elevate parts of the body for comfort.

Keep the bed as clean as possible. This means changing the sheets frequently. If the person sweats, vomits or does a lot of tossing and turning, you may have to change the bedding more than once a day. A rubber or plastic undersheet on top of the mattress will be useful. Having some towels to hand is a good idea as well.

If you need to change the sheets with the person in the bed, the safest and simplest procedure is shown below:

1. remove the top sheet

2. roll the person over to one side of the bed

3. cover them temporarily with a blanket or large towel

4. roll up the undersheet along their back

5. place the clean sheet over that part of the bed and tuck it in well

6. help them roll over onto the clean sheet

7. remove the undersheet completely and finish putting the clean one on

8. replace the pillow cases, put on a fresh top sheet and take away the temporary blanket or towel

Body care

As the person becomes weaker, you will have to
support them and help them move. You need to
learn the safest possible methods for doing this,
otherwise you will end up injuring yourself or them.
Bear in mind that it may be at this stage that care can
no longer be provided at home. They may need
constant specialist attention and professionals to
move them.

Before you start moving a person, or assisting
them in getting out of bed, you should ask the
visiting nurses to train you in the excellent
techniques and equipment developed to minimize
risk to both patient and carer.

Waste control

Most people are troubled if they soil themselves and
find it humiliating to have to rely on someone else to
enable them to go to the toilet. Physiotherapy
(which can be available to people at home as well as
in institutions) can be of great help in prolonging the
person's ability to move sufficiently to use a
commode near the bed.

Continence can be a major issue for a dying
person's self-image. Much depends on the attitude of
the carer. We are taught to regard the elimination
function of our bodies as repulsive. But excreting,
exhaling and sweating are the processes by which we
transform energies we no longer require. Try to care
for this aspect of a dying person with the same
dignity and tenderness with which you share the
other intimate and essential functions of their life.

Many techniques and products have now been
developed to help people relieve themselves in bed
or to cope with the loss of control over their
sphincter muscles. Seek the advice of the palliative
care team to find out what will be most suitable in
your circumstances.

Bathing

Regular washing is not only refreshing, but is important for skin care. If it is possible to take a bath or shower, a small stool in the bathroom may be helpful for either the person or the carer and for use in the shower if the person is unsteady on their feet.

Ask the palliative care team for advice on bed baths. It is important to ensure that the room is warm and that you have warmed the towels, water and damp cloths you will use to avoid chilling. Place a towel under the arm or leg you are washing. To get access to the back, roll the person on to their side, which also gives you a good opportunity to change the bedding (see pages 62–3).

After the bath use skin creams or lotions to keep the skin moist and prevent itching. If there is a problem with rashes, such as in the pubic region, dust with talcum or calendula powder. Health food shops and alternative health centres now stock a range of body oils and creams which have a range of properties that may be helpful.

Caring for the hair

Regular washing helps the scalp breathe and prevents itching.

Place the head just off the edge of the mattress. You can put a rubber or plastic sheet under the shoulders and down to the floor. Use a basin under the head.

Try "no rinse" shampoo or spray on powder shampoo for convenience. You can also experiment with organic and herbal shampoos available in health food shops and alternative health centres.

You could also take the opportunity to learn how to cut and care for hair. This is a wonderful way of communicating. If this is not possible for you, it is well worth considering visits from a hairdresser.

Common symptoms

Research into patients with advanced cancer has shown that most suffer from a cluster of common symptoms. These are thought to be associated to a greater or lesser extent with many other terminal illnesses. Although not everyone experiences these symptoms, carers should be aware that they might arise; that medication or advice from the palliative care/hospice team will help; and that complementary therapies and remedies are available.

Pain

The management of pain requires careful attention to all possible factors, including the person's physical, emotional, spiritual and social needs. Medication alone may not be sufficient.

Weakness

Most dying people find they are losing strength. Coming to terms with this can be extremely stressful, both for the person and their carers. Intense weariness and boredom are common. Physiotherapists aim to encourage a scheme of exercises to prevent weak people becoming bedbound and to help them restore a degree of mobility and independence.

Breathlessness

The feeling of being unable to breathe is very disturbing; those who experience it say they feel as though they are suffocating. The cause may be physical, but it can also result from being overwhelmed with anxiety.

Nausea and vomiting

Constant nausea and vomiting, which are both distressing and debilitating, can result from either the disease or the treatments. They may also signal powerful emotional disturbance.

Anorexia

Massive weight loss can be caused by the disease or its side-effects. This may well be helped by a very small dose of steroids. But weight loss may also reflect the fact that some people near death lose interest in food and give up the need to eat.

Constipation

Often ignored, this is one of the most common problems dying people face. It can contribute to many other conditions and be a source of much unexpressed and deep distress.

Confusion and depression

These states may set in at any stage in the illness. They may be made worse by inappropriate reactions from other people.

Other symptoms

Bedbound people may develop bedsores. They may experience paralysis, including impaired speech. Incontinence can be a major physical and emotional problem. Mouth sores, coughing and difficulty swallowing may also develop. All require immediate and appropriate attention.

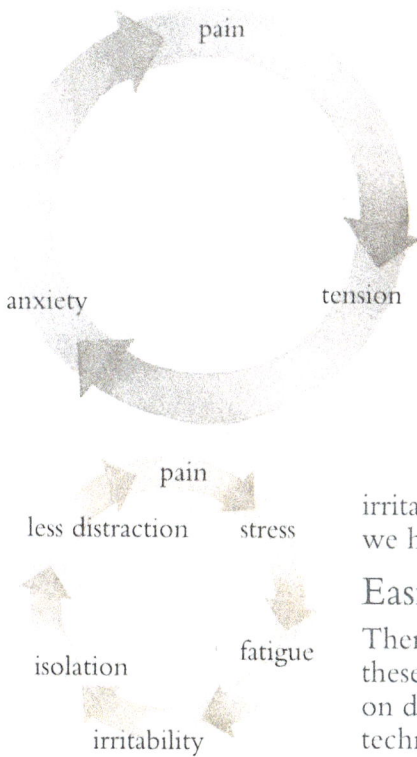

Vicious cycles

pain

tension

anxiety

pain

less distraction   stress

isolation   fatigue

irritability

Any injury or illness tends to create a spiral of pain, anxiety and tension. The cycle feeds on itself, with the anxiety and tension creating or intensifying painful sensations. This vicious cycle is common in people with terminal conditions and, even if there is little physical pain, the fear and anxiety often associated with dying may cause intense pain.

Stress increases with pain. The stress causes poor sleep and results in fatigue. The more enervated we are, the more irritable. This leaves us more isolated since people tend to avoid us when we are irritable. Without the diversion of human contact, we have little to distract us from our pain.

Easing the pain

There are a number of ways in which the effects of these cycles can be reduced without relying entirely on drugs. For example, various therapeutic massage techniques are used to reduce muscular and other pains and to encourage relaxation. Doctors specializing in pain relief have established that signals from the sensory nerves triggered by massage travel faster than those sent on the fibres that transmit ordinary pain signals in the body. The result is that massage actually alters the transmission of pain messages to the brain.

A relaxing massage reduces the overall level of tension that so often contributes to pain and has also been shown to activate the release of endorphins, the body's own pain killers.

Doctors have reported that massage has the additional advantage of helping patients deal with the sense of hopelessness and despair to which they often succumb.

Pain relief

In most forms of complementary medicine, pain is understood to be the result of a blockage in the natural circulation of vital energy in the body. This can be a localized blockage, often causing a specific pain, or the whole system of energy circulation can be weakened, causing a wide range of symptoms.

Because our fundamental energy is the basis of our mind and body, treatments which unblock or strengthen the flow of that energy address both emotional and physical manifestations of pain.

Herbal treatments

Herbal treatments can provide natural pain relief through their impact on the nervous system. They can be an excellent complement to other medication that may be prescribed. If you start using herbs, it is important to tell your doctor so that fact can be taken into account in your other treatments.

For the relief of intense pain, black cohosh is often recommended, as it is anti-inflammatory and has a powerful relaxing effect. Alternatively, you may find that passion flower or skullcap are helpful. Chamomile is often used by people who have a great sensitivity to pain and get easily irritated even by small pains. If you are experiencing sustained, immovable pain, a herbalist may recommend the use of Jamaica dogwood or pasque flower, after examination. Dosages will depend on whether you are experiencing acute or chronic pain.

See pages 26–7 for preparation of herbal teas and infusions. Instructions for use are normally provided at the point of sale.

❀

Aromatherapy for pain relief

•

use one or more of:
lavender
sweet marjoram
black pepper
or neroli
in a bath or massage.

•

Instructions for use are on pages 26–7.

❀

Natural painkillers

To deal with any form of pain and illness, it is important to strengthen the circulation of energy throughout the body. Natural remedies that can help include cinnamon, garlic, ginger, ginseng, watercress and wild oats. They can be added to your diet and drinks or used as infusions. For low energy that can lead to depression, try lemon balm, rosemary, St John's wort, skullcap, vervain or wild oats. If poor circulation results in confused states of mind, try gingko, ginseng, hawthorn, rosemary or wood betony. Instructions for use are normally provided at the point of sale.

The mind in pain

Pain is psychological as well as physical and our experience of pain is influenced by many factors. Sometimes, if we choose to, we are prepared to bear very high levels of pain. On the other hand, we many find much more minor pains unbearable. A great deal depends on our underlying beliefs about the meaning of pain and our mental and emotional reactions to specific pains. There are therefore many approaches to pain relief in addition to chemical (either synthetic or natural) painkillers.

1. Distraction
Some people find that their minds can be successfully distracted from dull, chronic pain for relatively long periods by listening to music, performing gentle exercises or getting involved in intricate handicrafts.

2. Counselling
For other people, skilled counselling can help ease their pain by reducing the stress levels which are part of the vicious pain–anxiety cycle.

3. Massage, acupuncture, TENS
Often people benefit from massage, acupuncture and the use of TENS (small devices that pass low electrical currents), which counteract the flow of pain signals in the nervous system.

4. Breath work
The two breathing exercises in this book on pages 88–9 and 148–51 have also been shown to help reduce the levels of pain and attendant anxiety.

5. Relaxation, meditation
The progressive relaxation exercise on pages 44–5 and the use of meditation (see pages 46–7) can affect the way we view pain and the way we react to it.

6. Visualization
Our mental power can be deployed in the fight against pain: sharp pain can be visualized as spikes of ice which we are slowly dissolving; dull pain can be imagined as pressure which we are slowly releasing; and deep pain can be seen as an intense red light which gradually changes to a pain-free white.

7. The inner smile
An ancient technique for pain relief is literally to smile into the area of the body where we think the pain is located. If we can learn to do this wholeheartedly, as if we were welcoming and befriending the pain unreservedly, remarkable changes are known to occur.

It is also possible to take a completely different view of pain. Some traditions believe it is our very effort to escape from pain that lies at the root of the suffering we experience. It is our stubborn resistance to pain and discomfort that leaves us in agony. The underlying emotional pattern that causes this resistance also affects our attitudes in many other areas of our lives. The practice, 'taking and sending', on pages 146–7 may prove helpful if you wish to explore this.

The warmth of human touch

Every one of us is a healer, because every one of us at least has a love for something.

EDWARD BACH

In the dark days of the military dictatorship in Chile, a mother was called to the emergency ward of one of the country's main hospitals. Her son had been detained by the security forces. They had poured petrol over him and set his whole body ablaze. He was now near death. Only the soles of his feet were unscathed. For hours his mother stayed with him, tenderly stroking his soles. It was the only part of his body that she could touch.

The scene is an indelible reminder of the suffering of an entire nation, but out of those flames there is also a lesson of hope for all who are caring for the dying. Perhaps the young man's mother could not have known it at the time, but of all areas of the body, the soles of our feet are one of the most sensitive to loving care. Countless nerve endings are found here as are many of the most important points used in acupuncture and reflexology.

Massage

Our hands, too, send and receive innumerable messages. Like our feet, they also record the history of our lives and you can tell a great deal about a person from studying and experiencing their hands. As an instrument of healing, our hands hold and express great power, and in the same measure, they are capable of receiving and interpreting the healing energy that comes to them from others.

Relatives and friends of a dying person can learn to massage each other's hands or feet instead of sitting helplessly round in hospital or at home. The massage becomes an act of loving tenderness that can be expressed and shared when words fail. This is one of the most powerful forms of communication. For people distressed by the suffering of a loved one, it offers a beautiful way to say with the warmth of human touch: "I care for you deeply".

Good massage practice begins with asking if the person would like to receive some massage, with an explanation of what will be done and with the person's explicit agreement. This is not always possible with people in the late stages of certain illnesses, in which case the carer needs to be as sensitive as possible to any signals that the person might not wish to be touched at certain times.

Reducing nervousness

People who are giving massage for the first time often feel nervous and self-conscious. You can use any of the relaxation or energy balancing exercises in this book before working on the person (pages 42–7). Have a warm drink and be sure your hands are warm before touching the person. Spend a little while sitting with them, just observing the vital rhythm of their breath, until the boundary between the two of you feels less distinct. Then focus on the kindly movements of the massage and don't be afraid to ask the person for feedback as you work.

Oils and powders

You may find that it is helpful to use a little oil (such as baby oil) or talcum powder to help lubricate your hands. This usually makes the rhythm of your hand movements smoother and more comforting. If that is not appropriate or possible for any reason, you can work gently without a lubricant.

Music or silence

Some people find it very relaxing to listen to soft music while they are being massaged. Others prefer silence. If you are in a position to have music, check to see if the person would like that and, if so, what.

Thin and dry skin

Some people are hesitant about massaging a person with thin, dry or fragile skin. In fact, the massage is helpful since it promotes circulation and lymph drainage and the oils lubricate skin tissues. You can adjust your firmness by asking the person to tell you how your massage strokes feel to them.

Hand massage

Since the person will be in very direct contact with your own energy field, always precede any hands-on work with the exercise 'balancing your energy' (see pages 42–3).

Holding the hand
Begin by simply holding the person's hand. Let your attention settle on their hand, notice the way it feels to you, what energy you sense in it and any nervousness or responsiveness. Let the boundary between your hands and their hand gradually soften. Take your time – it is extremely important not to rush this stage.

Opening the palm
Gently use your thumbs to squeeze and stretch their palm open until it feels softer and more pliant.

Pressing the palm
Work all over the palm, kneading every inch of the flesh with the pads of your thumbs. Where it is soft, work more deeply. Where there is resistance, work more gently. If bones and veins are close to the surface, press lightly.

Working around the wrist
Support the person's hand using both
your hands and use your thumbs to
work in small circles over the whole
wrist area. Turn the hand over and
work on the other side.

Stroking between the bones
Hold the person's hand so that the back
faces you. Use the thumb of your free
hand to stroke each of the grooves
between the bones of the hand, from the
webs between the fingers up towards the
wrist. Turn the hand over and stroke
between the bones in the palm.

Finger spirals
Enclose their thumb and each finger in
turn in your hand and gently pull them,
stretch them and slide your hand around
them in a spiral down and off the tip.

Pressure points
If the person is able to accept a little extra
pressure, you can produce a very satisfying
effect by working carefully around the
joints of each finger. With your thumb
and forefinger, squeeze the top and bottom
end of each joint, directing your energy in
towards the underside of the head of each
little bone in the finger. The angle of
penetration is shown in this drawing.
Work slowly down each finger from the
knuckle to the finger tip. Lean in to the
squeeze, so that you are putting your body
into the movement and not just the
muscles of your thumb and forefinger.

Foot work

You can seat the person in an armchair or sofa with the leg you are working on supported on a stool of similar height. If the person is bedbound you can adjust your own position at the bottom of the bed so that you have easy access to the soles of their feet. Rub a little talcum powder or oil on the feet.

Back and forth
Place the palms of your hands on either side of the foot, fingers relaxed. Now gently push forward with one hand and pull back with the other. Continue this movement alternately pushing and pulling their foot back and forth fairly rapidly, keeping your hands constantly in contact with the foot.

Ankle rotation
Support their heel in the opposite hand – right heel in left hand and vice versa – with your thumb around the outside of the ankle, just below the ankle bone. Now grasp the top of their foot in your other hand and gently rotate it a few times in one direction, then a few in the other.

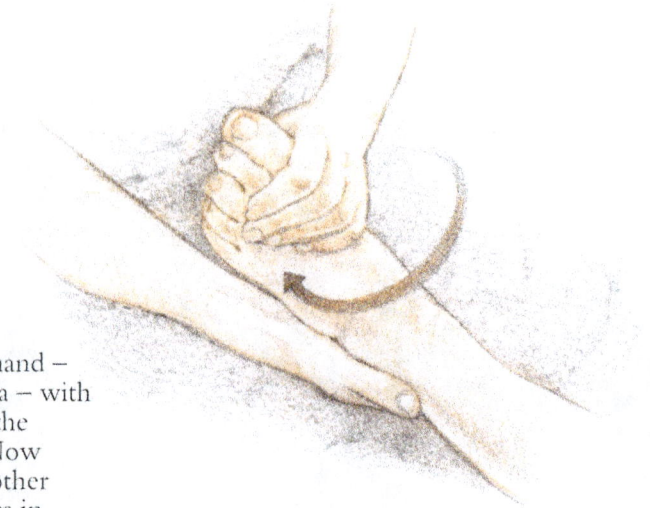

Stroking between the bones
Hold their foot with both hands. Use your
thumbs to stroke between the bones,
running from the toes up to the ankle.

Massaging the sole
Work all over the sole of their foot using
the heel of your hand to give firm pressure
fitting into each curve and bend of their
foot.

Supportive energy
If the person is able to accept pressure, you
can give them a little boost to their energy
by pressing a point in the sole of the foot
known in Chinese as Bubbling Spring. It is
one of the principal points through which
earth energy enters our being. You can
find Bubbling Spring by following a line
down from the middle toe to the indent
just behind the ball of the foot. Place the
pad of your thumb over the spot and relax
yourself using the procedure for 'balancing
your energy' (see pages 42–3). Then, as
you breathe out, lean in to the point for
5 to 10 seconds. Relax and breathe in.
Repeat up to five times.

Calming the stomach

The complex nature of many illnesses and the side effects of certain drugs often result in stomach problems such as nausea and vomiting. The problems may also be a manifestation of high levels of mental and emotional stress. The visualization and relaxation exercises in this book contribute to your need to be centred, stable and cared for and can sometimes be used very effectively to calm the disorder expressed by the stomach. You could try 'progressive relaxation' and 'balancing your energy' (pages 42–5) as well as 'mingling the breaths' (pages 148–9). All can be shared by carers and receivers.

❀

Aromatherapy for nausea and vomiting

•

use one or more of:
peppermint
ginger
lemon
caraway
or
sandalwood
in a bath or massage,
as an inhalation
or in a vaporizer.

•

Instructions for use are on pages 26–7.

❀

The Inner Gate

If a person is feeling nauseous, try pressing the energy point known as The Inner Gate. Pressure here calms the mind and harmonizes the energy of the stomach. First go through the exercise 'balancing your energy' (pages 42–3). Then locate the point by placing three of your fingers across the inside of the person's arm, starting at the crease of their wrist. The Inner Gate point is in the centre of their inner arm immediately above your three fingers. When you have located the point, relax and press in with your thumb for five to ten seconds as you breathe out. Release and breathe in. Repeat this sequence five times. Each time you press, imagine the sense of nausea departing along with the exhalation of your breath. Do this on the same point on both arms.

Herbal treatments

A number of herbs also contain properties that are beneficial in the treatment of nausea and vomiting. You can try any of the following, to see which one is most helpful: chamomile, cinnamon, dill, fennel, ginger, peppermint and rosemary.

Normally, patients are given medication to counteract the side-effects of chemotherapy. The stomach lining may be adversely affected. The herb slippery elm is extremely useful in protecting the lining of the stomach during chemotherapy and also in dealing with any other irritation of the gut.

See pages 26–7 for preparation of herbal infusions. Other instructions for use of herbs are normally provided at the point of sale.

Earth energy

The energy that comes to us from the earth has a direct connection with the energy of the stomach and is essential for our physical and emotional wellbeing. We draw energy from many sources and it is often our inability to connect with or absorb that energy which makes us susceptible to illness. The ailments associated with the stomach often have an emotional quality and may be related either to our need for nurture or to the depletion of our energy when we exhaust ourselves caring for another person.

Slow palming of the energy pathway connected to the stomach helps regulate the earth energies in the body.

1. Have the person lie comfortably on their back. If this is difficult, they can sit up allowing both legs to stretch out in front. Sit, stand or kneel beside them. First go through the exercise 'balancing your energy' (pages 42–3). Then firmly rest one hand on the person's lower abdomen. Keep that hand steady. Be aware of it, but don't lean into it: it is a connection point between the abdomen and the energy you will contact as you work with your other hand.

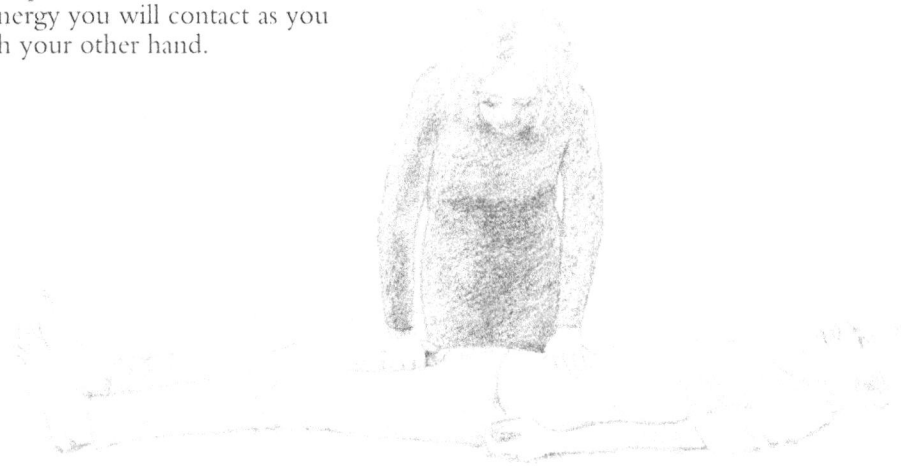

2. Place your other hand on the leg so that your palm covers the natural curve on the top outer edge of the thigh. As you breathe out, lean your weight gently towards the person so that your palm presses their thigh. As you breathe in, lean back and reposition your hand so that it is a little lower down the thigh. Exhale and lean in again. Do not press on the knee as this can be painful. Repeat this slow palming all down both thighs and calves.

3. As you lean in to the person, check that the pressure is bearable. If it is painful, move your hand along and repeat until you find an area which is comfortable when pressed. Some people can tolerate only very little pressure, so be sure to check with them as you do this.

Improving appetite

There are many reasons why people who are ill lose their appetite. In some cases it may be a direct result of the disorder from which they are suffering, or it may be a side-effect of the medication. Loss of appetite may have an emotional foundation as well. If a person becomes deeply depressed or anxious or has really given up their will to live, they may lose all interest in eating. Loss of appetite may also stem from a sense of distaste at their condition and the severe assault on their body-image caused by operations, weight loss and skin or hair disorders.

If you sense that the dying person is experiencing this kind of emotional trauma, you may find that massage can be of help to them (pages 68–73). This will be as true for them as it is for people suffering from anorexia at any age. The underlying cause may be lack of self-acceptance. Massage has been shown to be a powerful antidote to that, conveying acceptance, appreciation of the body and helping the person re-establish feelings of self-worth on a deep emotional level.

Bach flower remedies

The person may be suffering from a feeling of self-disgust or self-loathing. Even their own reflection in the mirror causes revulsion. They can no longer stand food and eating. In such cases, Crab Apple often proves effective. It is known as the "cleansing remedy" and like all the flower remedies it works on the emotional, rather than the physical level. Dr Bach described it as "the remedy which helps us to get rid of anything we do not like either in our minds or our bodies". Therefore, if the person's anorexia or other stomach disorders appear to stem in part from this emotional foundation, Crab Apple may be worth trying. Instructions for use are on pages 26–7 and are provided with all remedies at the point of sale.

❀

Aromatherapy for anorexia

•

use one or more of:
bergamot
caraway
or lemon
in a bath or massage
or as an inhalation
or in a vaporizer.

•

Instructions for use are on pages 26–7.

❀

Abdominal self-massage

Many complaints to do with the digestive processes are related to the stagnation of energy in the abdominal area. The resulting imbalance in one or more parts of the digestive tract leads to many illnesses and also to severe discomfort in the course of certain terminal conditions. The self-massage below can be used to energize and strengthen the entire digestive system, with corresponding positive effects on your circulatory and respiratory functions.

1. Before beginning the massage do the exercise 'balancing your energy' (pages 42–3). Then apply a little oil to your hands and gently rub them together until they are warm. This gives them greater power to influence the movement of energy (Chi) in your abdomen. If you prefer to do this massage without oil or keeping your abdomen covered, you may do so, but rubbing your hands together before beginning the massage is essential.

2. Place your hands, one on top of the other, over your navel. Start to make small, slow clockwise circles around your navel. Gradually make the circles larger and larger until your hands are around the entire outer rim of your abdomen. Make a total of 36 circular movements in all, evenly distributed over the area so that roughly a third are close to your navel, a third over the middle of the abdominal area and a third out towards the rim. Press firmly, but not too hard as deep pressure can be painful. Breathe naturally.

3. Having completed the 36 circles, place your hands directly above your diaphragm, just below your ribcage. Breathe in. Then, as you begin to breathe out, make your hands vibrate together up and down on that spot. Then, using the same vibrating action, slowly move your hands straight down to the lower rim of your abdomen. Breathe in and replace your hands over your diaphragm. Then, as you breathe out, repeat the same vibrating, downward movement. Complete 10 downward movements.

4. Finish by holding your hands over your lower abdomen, just below your navel for two minutes, breathing naturally.

Relieving constipation

Constipation is often related to the weakness of the energy associated with all forms of release and letting go, whether on a physical, mental or emotional level. Not surprisingly, it is an extremely common condition among dying people.

You can help relieve constipation by a technique known as colonic massage, because it affects the large intestine, or colon. The person must be willing to accept abdominal massage and not have a lesion (resulting from an operation) on the belly. The technique (called the Wave, see opposite) can be used as a form of self-massage or by a carer. Studies with elderly patients who frequently suffered constipation have shown an increase in the number of bowel motions after a period of gentle massage and in some instances the number of enemas needed was substantially reduced.

Many people have had operations in which a surgeon has made an incision in their abdomen. If you are caring for a person who has had such an operation, or has ascites, liver metastases or tumour mass in the area, do not attempt physical massage or pressure on their abdomen. Otherwise, see if a stomach massage helps relieve their constipation.

If the person does not like having their stomach massaged, or it is not possible because they have had operations in that area, you can influence the flow of descending energy by stroking the bottom end of their back.

Herbal treatments

Psyllium seed or linseed are gentle remedies which bulk our bowel contents and help push them along. Soak 1–2 teaspoons of seed in a cup of hot water for 2 hours. Add lemon and honey and drink at bedtime; if the problem persists have the drink in the morning as well.

Licorice is a natural laxative that can be taken either in the form of licorice root or in licorice sweets, but avoid it if there is high blood pressure or fluid retention. Yellow dock and burdock are more powerful laxatives and can be taken in an infusion along with equal amounts of licorice, ginger and dandelion root. The mixture can be taken 3 times a day.

Instructions on the preparation of herbal infusions are on pages 26–7. Other instructions for use are normally given at the point of sale.

❀

Aromatherapy for constipation

•

use one or more of:
bitter orange
black pepper
ginger
or
rosemary
in a bath or massage.

•

Instructions for use are on pages 26–7.

❀

The Wave

First go through the exercise 'balancing your energy' (pages 42–3).

1. Place one hand gently on the person's abdomen and rest your other hand on top of it.

2. Then with a wave-like motion, press gently down with the heels of your hand, followed by the middle of the palm of your hand and finishing with your fingers.

3. When your fingers press in, rock your hand back towards you a little and then begin a fresh wave motion starting with the heels of your hands.

4. Complete up to 10 of these wave-like movements.

Stroking the energy

1. Have the person turn onto whichever side is most comfortable for them.

2. Sit or kneel so that you can easily place the palms of your hands on the middle and lower part of their spine.

3. Rest both hands on the mid-section of their back. Go through the exercise 'balancing your energy' (pages 42–3).

4. Then slowly slide one of your hands down from the person's lower back to their tail bone. Exhale as you do so. Leave the other hand resting on the mid-section of their back.

5. Breathe in and return your moving hand to the small of their back. Then repeat, stroking downwards from the small of their back to their tail bone. You can do this for five to ten minutes.

Easing the breath

Breathlessness and other difficulties in breathing are common in people with serious illnesses, even if the main symptoms of the disease are connected with other organs. Breathing difficulties may worsen as the illness progresses.

Synchronized breathing and massage

Most forms of therapeutic touch are likely to have a beneficial effect on a person's breathing because they are so wonderfully relaxing. If the person tends to breathe in a very rapid and shallow manner, try encouraging slightly slower and deeper breathing while you are massaging their hands or their feet (see pages 70–3).

1. First synchronize your own breathing with your own massage strokes. Breathe in as your hands or fingers move towards your own body. Breathe out as the massage stroke travels in the outward direction.

2. Let the sound of your breathing be slightly audible. A natural interaction will occur and then with sensitivity you may find that you can help them relax into a naturally less distressed breathing pattern. This should be done without words, relying entirely on the interactive effect of the combined stroking and breathing. Do not tell the other person to change their breathing as that will only increase their anxiety, not reduce it.

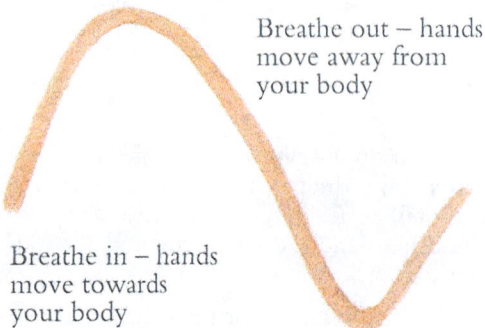

Breathe out – hands move away from your body

Breathe in – hands move towards your body

❀

Aromatherapy for breathlessness

•

use:
sweet marjoram
and frankincense
in a bath, as an inhalation
or in a vaporizer.

•

*Instructions for use are
on pages 26–7.*

❀

Herbal treatments

Breathlessness can have a number of causes, which can be diagnosed and treated by a trained herbalist. However, there are herbs you can use if you are aware of the related causes. If the root problem is weakness of the heart or poor circulation, garlic and hawthorn are recommended. If there is fluid retention in the lungs, try dandelion leaf tea. If the illness involves other chest problems, garlic, thyme or hyssop may prove beneficial. See pages 26–7 for preparation of herbal infusions. Other instructions for use are normally provided at the point of sale.

The sitting embrace

In the middle of the chest is an extremely important energy point, known as the Upper Point of the Sea of Energy. It regulates the energy of the lungs and helps relieve stagnation or tightness in the chest. It is located in the centre of the breast-bone, level with the nipples on a man.

1. To use this point, ask the person to sit up in bed or on a chair so that you can get access to both their chest and back. Position yourself comfortably and begin with the exercise 'balancing your energy' (pages 42–3).

2. Rest the palm of one hand on the centre of the person's chest. Place the 2nd, 3rd and 4th finger tips of your other hand together on one side of the person's spine, near the top of their back. Gently press in to the back as you breathe out. Feel that you are establishing a connection between these fingers and your palm on their chest.

3. Breathe in and relax. Then continue the pressing down to the mid-back. Then repeat going down the other side of the spine.

4. Finish by placing your palm on their back opposite your palm on their chest and imagine energy radiating between them for a minute as you breathe naturally.

Lifting the spirit

The dispersal of the body's energies can leave a person weak, exhausted and depressed. Sometimes this happens gradually, sometimes spasmodically. The result can be a state of great weariness. It may manifest itself physically, with the person simply lying back and drifting off to sleep, or mentally and emotionally, with a loss of interest in the people and events around them. Sometimes, there is much restlessness and fitfulness, reflecting the energetic imbalances in the body and nervous system. When this happens, the carers may also be sapped of vitality and succumb to deep depression.

Bach flower remedies

If the person's depression is the result of physical exhaustion, Olive is recommended. If the root of the problem is mental exhaustion, a sense that they simply cannot face the day ahead, then try Hornbeam.

There are other flower remedies associated with the relief of depression, depending on the nature of the person's suffering. Gentian helps to dispel negative thinking and is useful for temporary despondency brought on by setbacks such as an unsuccessful round of treatment. Gorse is recommended for those whose depression is deeper: they have given up hope and have no wish to carry on. In the most extreme cases of people experiencing desperate mental anguish, Sweet Chestnut is advised. It helps restore faith when people can see no way out of their inner darkness. They may feel so desolate and heartbroken that they physically hurt inside from emotional pain.

Instructions for use are on pages 26–7 and are provided with all remedies at the point of sale.

Heart-warming infusion
To strengthen the energy of
the heart and to sustain
warmth in the body,
prepare:
4 black peppercorns
4 cloves
4 cardamon pods
1 stick of cinnamon
a few slices of fresh ginger
in 1 pint (600ml) of water.
Simmer for 20–30 minutes.
Do not boil.
Cover to preserve the
volatile oils.
Use as a herbal tea or add a
tea bag to serve as spicy tea.
Sweeten to taste with honey.
Prepare with half milk, half
water if you prefer.
This infusion reinvigorates
the heart's power to circulate
energy in the body and to
harmonize the intense force
of our emotional reactions.

Herbal treatments

If a person is suffering from weakness following an infection, particularly from a virus, or needs to have their immune system strengthened, there are two herbs widely available that are worth trying. One is echinacea, also known as cone flower, the other is St John's wort. Echinacea is also recommended for all viral infections and allergies. To lift the spirit, try St John's wort, vervain, rosemary, lemon balm, skullcap, wild oats or thyme. See pages 26–7 for preparation of herbal infusions. Other instructions for use are normally provided at the point of sale.

Stabilizing the life centre

In many schools of Oriental medicine, the area around and particularly below the navel is treated as the vital centre of the body. It is here that we drew primal nourishment from our mothers' wombs. In Chinese medicine it is sometimes called the Sea of Energy. Holding this life centre can greatly help to calm a sick person and aid them in their own efforts to become more balanced. It often brings them considerable comfort.

1. Roll the person onto whichever side is more comfortable for them. Sit or kneel beside them (on either side and in any position which is comfortable for you), giving them support by bringing yourself right up beside their body. Stay still beside them for a minute and prepare yourself by silently going through the basic exercise of 'balancing your energy' (see pages 42–3).

2. Then place one of your hands over their lower abdomen, so that your thumb rests lightly on their navel and your fingers and palm naturally cover the area below. Place your other hand over the small of their back. Imagine your hands are like two heating pads and that a stream of warm energy is constantly passing between them. You can hold the person like this for as long as you wish. Your feeling will deepen as you hold them.

If the person suffers from shallow chest breathing, experiment with asking them to extend their abdomen outwards into your hand as they breathe in – as if the air was going right down to their belly. Then, as they exhale, their belly can subside. You can assist this movement by breathing with them in the same way, and letting your hands slightly guide the rise and fall of their abdomen. Be careful not to force this on anyone and if the person has no experience of this type of breathing, introduce it only very gradually, a few breaths a day.

❀

Aromatherapy for depression

•

use one or more of:
bergamot
Roman chamomile
clary sage
frankincense
lavender
or sandalwood
in a bath or massage, as an
inhalation or in a vaporizer.

•

*Instructions for use are
on pages 26–7.*

❀

Getting to sleep

Often sleeplessness is caused by too much energy rising to the head and upper body. Massage techniques that counteract this rise of energy, as well as herbs, oils and flower essences that calm the nervous system, have all proved useful in the care of dying people.

❀

*Aromatherapy
for insomnia*

•

use one or more of:
lavender
Roman chamomile
sweet marjoram
melissa
or
neroli
in a bath or massage, as an
inhalation or in a vaporizer.

•

*Instructions for use are
on pages 26–7.*

❀

Herbal treatments

Each person reacts a little differently to herbal preparations, and differently at different times. You may need to experiment a little with different herbs to see which is most useful as a night-time drink. Try preparing infusions using any of the following herbs to help with insomnia: chamomile, hops, lime flower, passion flower, pasque flower, Jamaica dogwood or wild lettuce. See pages 26–7 for preparation of herbal infusions. Other instructions on use are normally provided at the point of sale.

Bach flower remedies

White Chestnut is used when the mind is tormented all the time by worrying or repetitive thoughts. Dr Bach called this "the gramophone record remedy". It helps relieve the mental whirlpool and restore peace of mind. Agrimony is advised for people whose insomnia is associated with feelings and worries they suppress during the day, but which then emerge with greater intensity at night. These may be the sort of people who face all manner of difficulties with a brave and cheerful face, and never admit publicly to inner distress. Instructions for use are on pages 26–7 and are provided with all remedies at the point of sale.

Sleep pillow

Using dried herbs, choose a mixture of relaxing herbs such as lavender, hops, lime flower, chamomile and lemon balm, and add a few drops of neroli. Fill a small pillowcase or cushion cover with the herbs and place by your head or under your normal pillow so that you inhale the therapeutic aromas while you sleep.

The back stroke

The upward surge of energy in the body can be counteracted by stroking the person's back in the opposite direction.

1. Have the person lie on their side. Position yourself so that you can comfortably stroke their back. Then, in that position, go though the exercise 'balancing your energy' (pages 42–3).

2. Place your hand gently on the person's upper back.

3. Then slide it down to the small of their back, as you breathe out. Breathe in, relax and reposition your hand at the top of their back. Continue as long as you wish or until the person asks you to stop or falls asleep.

The cat stroke

1. Ask the person to lie on their front if possible, and bare their back.

2. Gently let your fingers trail down their back from the neck to the hips. Then let your other hand start stroking down the back, and keep up a slow, continuous cycle of stroking with alternating hands.

The motion has a calming, hypnotic effect on the nerves and usually produces a sensation of drowsiness. Allow the smooth, rolling sensation to develop and absorb both you and the person you are stroking. At the end, the strokes should become slower and lighter.

Stress relief

When we are under stress our body goes on an internal war footing. We become tense, our pulse rate and breath rate go up. You may not see the stress patterns but you can train yourself to identify them. Keep a diary: jot down the times when you get a headache, backache, when you suddenly feel a sense of panic or overwhelming exhaustion or when powerful emotions suddenly seem to sweep you away. Then go back and see what the circumstances were prior to each of these episodes. On the basis of what you discover, you can either take steps to prevent those circumstances or, if that is impossible, to follow the advice in these pages before the expected moments of intense stress.

❀

Aromatherapy for anxiety

•

use one or more of:
Roman chamomile
lavender
lemon
neroli
or ylang ylang
in a massage,
as an inhalation
or in a vaporizer.

•

Instructions for use are on pages 26–7.

❀

Children: stress and receptivity

If there are children around when someone is dying, or the child is themselves stricken with a terminal illness, it is important to bear in mind that they, too, suffer from stress. The stress reduction exercises on these pages can be used with children, as can the other practices and treatments elsewhere in this book. Children are often so open and receptive that they may derive even greater relief and inspiration from this type of work than adults. They can also be taught the basic massage techniques and, depending on their receptivity, help and inspire a dying adult through the guided inner work in Part Four.

Bach flower remedies

Stress can build up to such a level that sufferers have a desperate fear that their mind may give way. They may have the impulse to harm themselves, either during a sudden crisis or following a long period of depression and anxiety. Cherry Plum may be of considerable help (and is included in the Rescue Remedy, see page 165). Instructions for use are on pages 26–7 and are provided with all remedies at the point of sale.

Herbal treatments

Herbal medicine emphasizes the importance of strengthening a person's nervous system so that they are more naturally resilient to emotional pressures and better able to adapt in the face of life's crises. Vervain, taken as a herbal infusion, has a long history of use in this way, as do wild oats (usually taken as porridge or in flapjacks) and skullcap. Both licorice and ginseng increase the body's ability to deal with stress and prevent stress having a devastating effect on the organs and nervous system. The heart warming infusion on page 84 is also likely to be of considerable help.

Herbs recommended for their calming properties, and therefore useful in treating anxiety, include chamomile, lemon balm, passion flower and lime flower. These are all commercially available in herbal teas and instructions for preparation of herbal infusions are on pages 26–7.

Breath work

By adjusting the speed of your breathing, you can reduce the agitation in your nervous system.

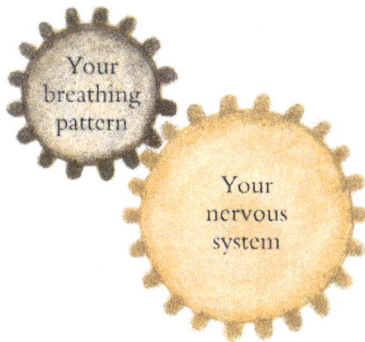

Your breathing pattern

Your nervous system

Nervous activity and anxiety will cause your breathing to speed up, and will be calmed by changes in your breathing.

If you feel yourself becoming anxious or tense, the following simple breathing exercise can bring you some relief. It works by using the rhythm of your breathing pattern to send a "calm down" signal to your nervous system. Greater attention is paid to the exhalation (out-breath) since this is when your diaphragm relaxes.

You can do this exercise on your own, but this is often difficult under severe stress. In that case, ask someone to read you the instructions as often as necessary.

1. Start by taking as big a breath as you can comfortably.
2. Then, as you breathe out, release the air fully from your lungs.
3. At the end of the breath, relax your shoulders – they often tighten up when we are tense.
4. Repeat the cycle of inhalation and deep exhalation at least three times.
5. Continue as long as you wish, placing most of your attention on breathing out and relaxing your shoulders. Your eyes may be open or closed.

Mutual breathing

The exercise, 'mingling the breaths', on pages 148–9, can be used during any period of tension or pain. If the person's breath rate shoots up, stay close and synchronize your breathing with theirs. Emphasize your out-breath. Once you are riding their rhythm, gradually lengthen your own out-breaths, as if gently drawing their breath rate along with yours.

Stay with the person as long as necessary. If you feel dizzy or tired, pause to regain equilibrium or work in relays with someone else.

This technique can often have a remarkable effect, bringing pulse rates down from as high as 164 beats a minute to 76 beats a minute within 20 minutes.

You begin to work with the person's breath rate following it and slowly lengthening it.

rapid breathing

| 5 minutes synchronised breathing at rapid rate | 5 minutes slight lengthening of out-breath | 5 minutes further lengthening of out-breath | 5 minutes synchronised breathing at slower rate |

Relieving tension and confusion

Throughout any period of illness our brain is assailed with what it perceives as abnormal and confusing data from our organs and nervous system. If there is no opportunity to relax, it finds it increasingly hard to regulate all the processes it must deal with. A state of tension ensues and is reflected throughout the body.

Relaxing the head

A great deal of tension is stored in the facial and other muscles of the head. Therapeutic massage affects not only the immediate skin and muscles here, but the entire nervous system.

Begin by going through the exercise 'balancing your energy' (pages 42–3). Make yourself comfortable and warm your hands. Use a little oil on your fingers if you wish.

As you make the massage movements below, you will achieve far better results if you imagine that you are working below the surface of the skin. This does not mean that you need to apply extreme pressure, but rather that you create a feeling in yourself that your touch is gently penetrating to a deeper level in the person.

❀

Aromatherapy for confusion

•

use one or more of:
frankincense
petitgrain
rose otto
or
sandalwood
in a bath, as an inhalation
or in a vaporizer.

•

*Instructions for use are
on pages 26–7.*

❀

1. Forehead
Rest your thumbs above the eyebrows on either side of the midline of the forehead, with your hands anchored on the sides of the head. Lean in gently and, breathing out, slowly slide your thumbs towards the temples. Then move your thumbs up slightly and repeat until you have covered the entire forehead.

2. Eyebrows
Beginning with the inner end of the eyebrows, firmly slide your thumbs along the hair, just as you did for the forehead movements. You can also grip the flesh of the eyebrows between your thumbs and forefingers and knead it, again starting nearest the midline and working outwards.

3. Ears
There are numerous acupuncture points in the ears and slow, careful work over the entire ear surface can be very rewarding. Grasp the ears between your fingers and thumbs, and experiment with squeezing and stroking them.

Standing like a tree

An ancient Chinese internal energy exercise (Chi Kung), known as Standing Like a Tree, is excellent for calming the entire nervous system. It is normally done standing, but the same principles can be applied for a weaker person who may need to stand with their back resting against a wall or be sitting up in a chair. The stationary positions promote increased circulation and deeper breathing, and induce inner calm.

1. Simply stand with your feet shoulder width apart. Unlock your knees slightly. Let your arms rest effortlessly by your sides. Relax your shoulders. Breathe naturally. Keep your eyes open and look calmly forward. Try remaining quietly in this position for a minute or two to begin with and gradually build up to several minutes if possible.

2. As you stand in the position, imagine that your feet are like the roots of a great tree sinking down into the earth. Your body remains unmoving like the trunk of the tree. You imagine that the very top of your head is lightly suspended from a golden cord reaching up infinitely into the sky; it is as if your head was as relaxed as the countless leaves of the tree opening into the sunlight.

3. You can try a variation on this exercise if you are in bed. Lie flat with your legs slightly separated. Flex your feet so that your toes are nearly at right angles to your legs. Imagine you are holding a large balloon in your arms, over your stomach. Try to stay in that position for a short while, relax and repeat whenever you wish.

For further information on internal energy exercises see Resources, page 186.

Spiritual care

It is often thought that the spiritual needs of the dying are the unique province of priests, psychologists, death counsellors or other specialists. Not so. The spiritual care of the dying is a shared task. At its heart is the person who is dying. They share their deathwork with all those to whom they have been close in life and eventually with all those who come into contact with them and assist them in dying.

Those who work with dying people find that neat, professional, intellectual or religious answers are often not what is being sought.

As Dame Cicely Saunders, the founder of the hospice movement, wrote: "The dying have shed the masks and superficialities of everyday living and they are all the more open and sensitive because of this. They see through all unreality. I remember one man saying: 'No, no reading. I only want what is in your mind and in your heart.'"

Honesty and openness

By their presence, by their suffering, through their silences and their utterances, the dying invite us to encounters of complete honesty and openness. It is our willingness to enter into those encounters that constitutes authentic spiritual care. These are encounters of unfettered human energy. They embrace our anger, our fears and hopes, our depression and our acceptance. Nothing is excluded, nothing is regarded as less than human or less than sacred.

If you are asked about life's meaning and have no answer, say so. If you have an answer, give it freely. What matters is the willingness to open fully to that person and to accept them as they are, unconditionally. If we are willing and able to respond in that way, they are able to complete their life's work and to enrich us by the power of their death.

The endless knot embodies the interdependence of all life and all beings. Our presence – just being ourselves – is itself the presence of all that exists, of all wisdom and all love.

"I'll hold the rope while you scale the depths of the cavern"

EDITH CAMPBELL, a chaplain to people suffering from HIV and AIDS in New York:

"You are accompanying the person on a journey. You are travelling in unknown territory together. What the person needs is not to be told what to look at and what is beautiful or to have things explained to them. What you are able to do is to help clear the way so that person on the journey is able to tell you what they see, is able to point out to you the fullness and the beauty and the strangeness of the territory that they are going through.

It takes mutual cooperation to enable that to happen. You need a relationship of trust and openness, shared humanity, the understanding that this person is there as a full human being with you in your full humanity.

We are struggling in the midst of this to make sense of what we are going through. It requires you to let go. It's about surrendering all of your ideas about what you think you have to offer and listening to what that person is really asking you for. Often what they want most is just another person to be alongside them in the midst of this, to acknowledge that this is scary and frightening.

I'm frightened too, because I don't have the answers. What I have is what little I have. I'll be there with you as much as I can. You are not alone. I'll hold the rope while you scale the depths of the cavern. I won't let you go, but I cannot go into that cavern with you. I'm here. I'm here at the top of the rope and I'll help bring you up as much as I can.

Just knowing that someone else is there is the greatest gift you can offer to someone going through all of that, to make the space, to provide an environment where the person can go into their own journey more fully."

The golden orb

In the dark days of World War II, a young German officer who was working secretly against the Nazis was arrested and subjected to brutal interrogation. As he faced his tormentors, he was suddenly seized with the miraculous sense of being surrounded with golden light. He felt nothing but inner calm as the globe of light protected him. After days of sustained questioning he was released unharmed.

Years later he was to become one of Europe's leading specialists in the use of light and colour in the treatment of disease and the care of the dying. "The biochemical structure of the human being is deeply affected by vibrations of all sorts, including the frequencies of the light spectrum," he advises.

Illness weakens our protective energies, making us both more sensitive and more vulnerable. This means that we are open to positive influences to which we may have previously been closed, as well as to vibrations which may disturb us.

Golden light has a protective and supportive quality which can be extremely beneficial under these circumstances. Golden tints in fabrics such as curtains or bed covers are a way of providing this protective environment.

Blue light has a deeply relaxing power which has been shown to be of great help to people suffering from fear and anxiety. For example, blue silks, pyjamas or bed clothes can induce this relaxing effect.

If a person has difficulty sleeping because of the anxiety they are experiencing, you can try placing a night light in the room consisting of a daylight colour light bulb enclosed in full spectrum blue stained glass. If this is not possible, experiment with having the person visualize blue light as they breathe in and its complementary colour, orange, as they breathe out.

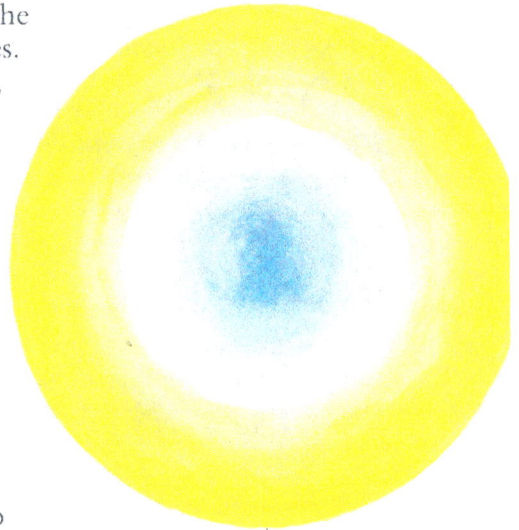

The visualization

The orb is covered on the outside with protective gold. At its heart is a sphere of blue light which is totally free from fear and anxiety. Imagine yourself suspended inside this three-dimensional sphere. Once you are familiar with the image, try to hold it in your mind's eye and feel yourself immersed in it. This exercise can be profoundly nourishing to anyone who is seriously ill or weak; it drains no energy from them.

The great harmonics

Our ability to hear is fully functional for several weeks before birth and is usually the last physical sense to leave us. As we approach death, our hearing becomes unusually acute: it appears to have a special power in the transition of consciousness from one state to another. There is evidence that even when a person is unconscious, the hearing function is undisturbed: patients retain memories of comments in the operating theatre, overheard while anaesthetized.

This phenomenon lies at the heart of the ancient death practices which involve talking the person through the experience of death and afterwards. It also underlines the way in which we can use sound, and particularly music, to ease and accompany the transformations which the person is undergoing.

From the earliest times, teachers and healers have understood sound to be a sacred, primal form of energy. Sickness and disease are seen as an "untuning" of some part of the wonderful musical pattern of life. Sound can be used to retune the frequencies depleted by disorders of the body and can be used to strengthen the wholesome resonances of the whole person's vibrational field.

Sound therapists often use the healing power of music to help people overcome emotional roots of destructive pain, grief and anger since it can be very powerful in transforming their deep sense of isolation. In some countries, specialized groups now offer a remarkable service of "musical midwifery" for the dying: they support the person by holding them and singing while accompanied on small Celtic harps.

It is also possible to experiment with recordings from the natural world, such as water sounds or natural pipe instruments, which have a uniquely lyrical and relaxing quality and evoke our profound connection with the life force.

Experience has shown, however, that intervening periods of silence or relative quiet are equally important since the mind of the person is often engaged in inner reflection and interior listening.

Listening and talking

Something terrible happens when we stop the mouths of the dying before they are dead. A silence grows up between us then, profounder than the grave. If we force the dying to go speechless, the stone dropped into the well will fall forever before the answering splash is heard.

FAYE MOSKOWITZ

A very common first reaction among people confronted with death or a dying person is: "I don't know what to say." The truth is that not only may you have nothing to say, but what you say is not the real entry point for the journey. The first question to ask yourself is: "Do I know how to listen?"

A dying person often goes through phases, alternating between speech and silence. Visitors and carers may be so obsessed with doing or saying something nice that they end up trying to have a conversation when the person needs tranquillity, or else they bustle around when the person needs someone to stop and listen to them.

Tuning in to the dying person is the key to preventing this mismatch. It requires a willingness to go beyond your own agenda and timetable and even your own compulsive desire to be helpful. You start to create open space by simply spending time with the person with no other purpose in mind. You are just there.

Space and meaning

Our conventional response is to rush into any vacuum, to give the person our own thoughts to comfort them. That is helpful if specifically asked for, but a far richer dialogue flows from the effort to draw the other person out and to understand the significance of what they are saying. Their insights are unique and may be of inestimable worth to those who listen. In the words of an old saying, "When you speak you say only what you already know; when you listen, you learn."

Those who work with the dying emphasize the importance of letting the person control the pace and content of communication. The rush of our own reactions often gets in the way. "What is needed is the space to explore the dimensions of the situation

An essential part of good caring is not making assumptions about what is important to the person, and being sensitive to their changing needs.

People with a terminal illness sometimes find other people treat them as if they were in mental quarantine. Why assume that the person has lost interest in the world around them, doesn't want to know the latest news or gossip, and doesn't have views on what is happening? Often shared reminiscences are of great value, too, letting the person know how their life influenced others and thereby reinforcing their personal sense of meaning.

that arises when one is confronted with a life-threatening situation," advises one worker, "to explore the meaning, the confusion about life and death and what lies beyond, if anything."

Uncertainty and communication

Whether you are dying or helping a dying person, you are living with extreme uncertainty. Normally we are able to create and cling to apparent certainties – even if these are only illusions. But death strips them away. Even the effort to establish certainty in the face of death creates additional anxiety. It is best to face up to this reality.

Realize from the outset that literally everything can change from moment to moment, from day to day. Don't frustrate yourself by demanding consistency.

Ask open-ended questions and probe the meaning of the answers. Don't overlay questions and answers with your own assumptions.

Be willing to accept "I don't really know" as an answer and to accept the fact that this may be your own answer to many questions.

Be open about the uncertainty of the situation with others. Don't assume you must carry any burden on your own. Seek advice and support openly.

Always remember that a dying person is a living person in a crucial phase of their existence. Respect their individuality, their experience and their autonomy.

Beyond language

The dying person may no longer be able to converse. But that is not the end of communication. A man sitting at the bedside of his silent dying mother later wrote these words:

"I felt powerless, small and helpless, but also peaceful, strong and quiet. I was seeing and feeling something I had never seen or felt before, an experience that to be described would require words that have not yet been found: powerless, yet strong, sad yet peaceful, broken yet whole. Everything was truthful. We experienced the privilege of being close to her suffering, intimately connected with her pain. I have never felt so strongly that the truth can make us free."

Silence and saying what you mean

In the depths of the Amazonian rainforest, when death comes to a member of the community, the family is joined by a tribal shaman who guides them through the final phase of the person's life. Widely misrepresented as "witch doctors", shamans are respected in indigenous traditions as mediators between the human realm and the mysteries of the universe. The distinguishing mark of all shamans, by whatever name they are known, is fearlessness in the face of death.

In our industrialized culture, such figures are rare. Yet if we are to die well ourselves and be of the greatest help to those who are dying, that is what we must become: people who are clear-eyed in the midst of death. We are then at peace with our own mythology.

To accomplish this, two fundamental qualities are required. You must be completely at ease in silence. You must feel completely free to say what you mean.

These abilities are not magical or esoteric skills. They do not require a "spiritual personality". We are all born with them. They are so simple we constantly overlook them. And yet they are the foundation of the most profound insight and love we can share with each other.

Death holds no terrors for us. We meet it with simplicity and perfect calm, seeking only an honourable end as our last gift to our family and descendants.

OHIYESA OF THE
SIOUX PEOPLE

Natural wisdom

Rediscovering how to rest in natural silence may at first seem difficult and anything but natural. We are swept away by constant agitation and by the intensity of the emotions we feel. We need to anchor ourselves in the midst of that, be fully aware of all the disturbances around us and yet not be incapacitated by them. An ancient method for anchoring ourselves is to listen to our bodies (see "The body of wisdom", pages 42–3). Once we have that anchor, and have returned to a sense of equilibrium in ourselves, nature takes over: we stop babbling and regain the innate ability to express ourselves simply and straightforwardly when needed.

Working with the professionals

Death is difficult terrain for health professionals. They react to it with the same emotions that the rest of us do. But it is all the more difficult for them, since the death of a patient is often regarded as a failure. Indeed, doctors take the Hippocratic Oath which obliges them "to treat, to cure and to prolong life".

Not only do terminal illnesses defy the medical ideology of finding a cure for all conditions, they are characterized by constant uncertainty – at the very time when patients and family are often demanding definite answers and predictions about the course of the illness.

Sick people are often unhappy with the way health workers communicate with them. The medical jargon is unfamiliar and many professionals avoid speaking openly about emotionally sensitive subjects. Various studies have shown that health workers often fear their patients' diseases and may shield themselves emotionally from dying people.

All these factors complicate communication between professionals and the people they are caring for.

Science says: "We must live" and seeks the means of prolonging, increasing, facilitating and amplifying life, of making it tolerable and acceptable; Wisdom says: "We must die" and seeks how to make us die well.

MIGUEL DE UNAMUMO

Researchers have identified four styles of communication between health professionals and their clients. These can also apply to dying people and their friends or family members.

Openness. The dying person and the other person know what is happening and are open about it.

Suspicion. The dying person suspects what is happening but says nothing about it.

Mutual pretence. Both know that the other person knows but say nothing about it to each other.

Closed. The dying person does not know what is happening and the other person is certain of this and says nothing to the contrary.

Another observation is that the dying drift in and out of the awareness of dying – sometimes acknowledging it, sometimes not. Instead of asking, "Does the dying person know?", it may be more appropriate to ask "When, with whom and how does the person address the issue of dying?".

Dying people give clues to their carers about what they know and want to know. However, it is important to be sensitive to the fact that some people prefer to remain closed and to have that personal choice respected.

In the midst of the confusion

What can you do to ensure effective communication with professionals, either as a dying person yourself, or as a carer for a dying person?

Try to be as clear and precise as possible. If you don't understand what is being said to you, ask until you do. A good method is to repeat back to the professional, in your own words, what you think has been said and check if your understanding is correct.

Get a proper notebook in which you or someone else can keep a written record of what you are told. If you are having trouble taking information in, ask the professional to write the information in your notebook. You can also use the notebook to list the questions you want to ask. Treat this like your medical diary, so you have a clear record of everything in one place, including names, dates, telephone numbers and all important messages relating to the illness and treatment.

Remember that you have every right to seek the information and advice you need in order to understand what is happening and to take intelligent decisions.

Whenever you are confused or uncertain, say so. If you need time to reflect, be clear about that.

If there are cultural considerations or traditions that you want respected, or if there are particular aspects of your lifestyle that are important to preserve as far as possible, make these crystal clear to any professional you are dealing with and make sure that you are being heard.

Your circumstances, your condition and your feelings are likely to change from day to day. Don't feel under any pressure to be consistent. Be as open and honest as you feel is appropriate from day to day; this is the best way to help the professionals understand your changing needs.

PART THREE

The great storm

EMOTIONS

·

ATTITUDES

·

INTIMATE NEEDS

The greatest discovery of my generation is that human beings can alter their lives by altering their attitudes of mind.

WILLIAM JAMES

Your death mythology

To the ancient Greeks, three daughters determined the inescapable destiny of every mortal. These were the Fates. One spun the thread of each person's life. One was the element of luck. And when the third cut the thread, death was certain.

As with the Greeks, every culture has its mythology of death. Each person, too, has their own. By "mythology" it is important to understand not something that is false or fantastic, but a deep pattern of belief and imagery which lies at the very foundation of our attitudes, emotions and reactions to events.

The pattern of our personal mythology may coincide with, or be derived from, a major religion. It may be rooted in the widely held views and common sense of the society in which we live.

It may be intensely private, shaped by our very earliest experiences, and possibly unacknowledged even to ourselves.

Signposts

It is not all that easy to gain access to your own underlying mythology. Much of its power lies in remaining hidden from view.

We hear echoes of our own mythologies when we react to the deaths of others. It is often difficult to know whether we are expressing our own convictions or simply falling back on well-worn formulae:

The body is a machine which wears out. That's all there is to it, really.

It was fate. Looking back, you can see it was inevitable.

This is such a tragedy. It makes you wonder what the point of living is.

It is so unfair, so unjust.

It is God's will.

Whether we use such statements intentionally or casually, behind each lies a view of life. That world view is ever-present, and will determine how we react to our own deaths and to the death of every single person we know.

In the last analysis it is our conception of death which decides the answers to all the questions that life puts to us.

DAG HAMMARSKJÖLD

Inner journey

You start to encounter your own mythology when you are told you are dying, when someone you love dies, or when you have to care for a dying person. Death's utterly uncompromising character forces you back onto the very foundations of your existence. What you discover there is unique to you and you embark upon an inner journey. This is true whether your response to the onset of death is complete resistance or complete acceptance. It is true whether you start off utterly confused, shot through with anger and pain, numbed by despair or spiritually uplifted.

It is possible to gain access to your mythology of death and test it in advance of such experiences. You can ask yourself about the overall framework in which you react to death:

For you, is death part of a far larger divine scheme? A purely medical phenomenon? Is it something you accept willingly as part of nature?

Do you have an idea of how you would like to die? How important is it to you to be able to control your own death?

Is there an age at which you feel it would be appropriate to die?

Can you sum up your reactions by drawing a picture of what death means for you?

The changing bedrock

Although our mythology is deeply embedded and so many of our habits of mind rest on it, the curious thing about it is that it can change at any moment. Intense emotional experiences can affect elements of our mythology so rapidly that our habitual reactions suddenly seem hollow and no longer adequate to express what we feel. This malleable quality of our inner world also means that it is possible to create or influence our private mythologies and literally prepare ourselves in advance for certain crises in our lives.

Losing control

Our personal mythology is part of our strategy for controlling our experience. We spend a great deal of our lives trying to stop things falling apart. When they go wrong, we find ourselves struggling with our emotions, and searching for someone to blame. We don't like to be told that if we had approached things differently with realistic expectations, we wouldn't be going through the same pain.

Death brings this control pattern into the sharpest possible focus. When death enters our lives it totally negates our ingrained quest for security. We cannot take it in. We are confused and enraged; we turn to the wall in despair; we are reduced to our most primitive behaviours. Believing at a subliminal level that we could somehow always retain control, we find ourselves unprepared for the full force of reality.

What you can control

Although you may not be able to control the forces that shape your life, you are not completely powerless. You can reorient your expectations and reactions so that you are better equipped to handle shock.

Studies have shown that very high levels of stress are generated by people who try to escape or deny the uncertainty they face. This is true of all those involved in anyone's death. It is better for everyone to acknowledge openly the many uncertainties in the situation. This frank admission places everyone on a more honest footing and encourages an atmosphere of trust.

Some types of uncertainty can be avoided. The way we talk to each other in times of stress makes a difference. Sometimes we use vague terms, assuming that uncertainty is less painful than "bad news". But this assumption can lead to extremely distressing situations of confusion and mistrust. Particularly when we are involved in decisions on matters of life and death, it pays to find out what everyone really means. In one study, doctors were asked what they meant when telling a patient they had a "real chance". One doctor said it meant a one per cent chance, another a 99 per cent chance!

Our feelings

Losing control may make us feel:

frustrated

angry

vengeful

anxious

fearful

confused

sad

depressed

guilty

helpless

isolated

We may be thrown into such a state of shock that our only defence is denial.

We may experience other feelings — and bodily sensations — not listed here, and our responses may vary and be unpredictable.

Controlling our world

The ancient Chinese thought the world rested securely on the stable back of a giant tortoise.

For centuries, Western civilization clung to the model of a flat earth under the heavens.

Even the early 20th-century model of the atom has been overtaken by Heisenberg's Uncertainty Principle since it is not possible to locate any atomic particle simultaneously in time or space.

The desire to find or impose order on our world is one of the most deep-seated tendencies in human nature. It is one way in which we seek control. Each of these models served its purpose in its day, but the exploration of outer space and the examination of the subatomic universe now show the cosmos itself to be far larger, and more contradictory and uncertain than we previously supposed. We make similar efforts to explain and control even the smallest details of our daily lives. But life and death force us constantly to rethink.

IN THE MIRROR

The world around us is constantly telling us that there are limits to what we can control. We tend to find these messages frightening and ignore them, or we strengthen our defences and tighten up. The effect is to make inevitable events like illness, ageing and death all the more threatening and disorienting. Our investment in security can also put a straitjacket on our approach to life itself. Ask yourself:

What investment of time, money and energy do you put into making your life secure?

How do you react to the ordinary crises and calamities you face at home and in your work?

Are there ways in which you over-control not only your own life, but the lives of others as well?

If you had only a short time to live, would that change your perspective and need for control?

In the laboratory

One day in the early years of investigating the atom, the international team of scientists that was being assembled in the United States looked up to see one of their European colleagues walking into the laboratory wearing large pink fluffy bedroom slippers. His face was ashen. "Why have you got those on your feet?" they asked. He replied: "I'm afraid of falling through the floor. It's going too fast."

His world had spun out of control. All the matter that he and his fellow scientists had previously understood to be solid was now seen to be a vast, unpredictable cloud of energy and emptiness. Their discoveries had destroyed all their assumptions about the world – and it was terrifying.

We go through this same sense of dizziness and fear when our own certainties are shaken. The more dependent we are on them, the greater the vertigo when they disappear. Even if we know them to be illusions, it is deeply unnerving when they are shown to be false and are blown away.

Falling away

As the ground falls away from under us, we experience the full force of our anxiety. Fears have a shape, but anxiety is more formless. Anxiety is a state of being. We are unsettled in ourselves. We are apprehensive. We cannot depend on our mind: it wanders. Our reactions are nervous and we become obsessive, sometimes about little details. Sleep does not come easily to us. We are often fatigued, as if we were constantly looking for something we had lost and cannot find.

Although we encounter this state to some extent when confronted with the death of anyone, if we examine ourselves closely we recognize it as being more pervasive than the fear of death itself. Indeed, what we say we fear is what we are aware of and prepared at that moment to admit to. But beneath it lies this other shapeless, anonymous sensation, as if our lives were spinning slightly off centre.

In one of the few large-scale surveys of attitudes to death in Europe, people were asked what would make the thought of death less painful. A quarter emphasized religious beliefs, a further quarter stressed the building of significant relations with other people or having children, and of the others who responded positively, the majority said the difference would be made by leading a satisfying life or working towards their ideals.

The pain–anxiety spiral

Anxiety is frequently associated with acute pain. The anxiety itself can greatly intensify the pain experienced, as numerous hospital studies have established. Our pain sensations often increase as a result of our reaction to loss of control over our bodily functions, of our anticipation of pain and of inaccurate expectations we may harbour about what will happen to us.

The pain–anxiety spiral can often be dealt with very effectively (provided we wish to be treated in this way) if:

we are provided with accurate and timely information about our condition, treatment and side-effects

we are included in decision-making

we are supported psychologically and emotionally.

Meeting these needs will support everyone involved by helping them accept and deal with the real uncertainty of their situation, rather than trying to impose artificial certainties on it. Our anxiety and other feelings are legitimate, not because they are necessarily logical, but simply because they exist. Our feelings are not the problem. Our problem is how to accept them, express them and use them.

IN THE MIRROR

In the same way that many thinkers tell us that death and life are inextricable, it may be that our anxiety about death is in fact a more fundamental anxiety about life. We devise countless ways of evading it, until death, our mirror and teacher, removes our defence. If we have done nothing but run away all our lives, we are ill-prepared for that encounter with ourselves. You can ask yourself:

How does the sensation of anxiety manifest itself in your life?

Is it purely related to the thought of dying?

When you experience anxiety, what are your typical responses?

Have you developed any way of tolerating or living with anxiety that is not an escape from it or a denial of it?

The splinters of fear

The fear of death has an irresistible magnetism. We are drawn to it, motivated by it and appalled by it. Its power over us is fundamental to our existence. It triggers our entire nervous system at even the slightest threat and, moment after moment, it drives the life functions of our internal organs.

Yet, for all its power, the fear of death is elusive. If we ask ourselves what exactly we fear about death, what seemed so overwhelming in its implacable solidity begins to break apart. The fear of death splinters into a composite of many fears.

When you are told you have a medical condition from which you may not recover, fear ranges across a broad spectrum. Much of it is brought on by the loss of control over yourself, your environment and the unfolding events of your life. There is a fear of becoming helpless. Associated with this is the fear of deterioration and the loss of personal dignity.

Some people are extremely distressed by the thought of being a burden to others. Mixed in with the loss of control may be deep-seated worries about unfinished business, including unresolved emotional issues – and the fear that addressing these will open Pandora's Box precisely when we are running out of time and can no longer control situations.

The unknown

Many of us are afraid, not only of the pain of the illness, but of the medical treatment to which we may be subjected. Requiring treatment may represent failure and the fear of it, cowardice. At a time of maximum vulnerability, we are thus threatened with the fear of being "exposed" as failures and cowards at the end of our lives. The unknown looms large, including for some the terrifying prospect of oblivion, for others judgment after death. It is precisely in the face of these overwhelming uncertainties that so many dying people express the fear of dying abandoned, of being left to face the final moment alone.

It is not death that is the source of all our evils, and of a mean and cowardly spirit, but rather the fear of death.

EPICTETUS

We believe we fear death. That fear holds sway over our lives. But if asked what it is we really fear, we begin to wonder if it is death we fear, or something else. It is as if, behind the vast army of fears, there were another power that holds us in its spell.

Death fears

Studies of people's death fears suggest that it is possible to construct a list of our most common concerns. A list of your own fears might include some of the following, or others not in this list:

leaving behind everything and everyone we have loved

losing control over our own lives

leaving important personal commitments unfinished

experiencing prolonged illness, pain or violence

losing our personal and bodily dignity

becoming a burden to others

deteriorating physically and mentally

being judged in this life or in the hereafter

disappearing into an abyss of annihilation

The relatives of the dying person may share many of these fears. They may also fear being a survivor, faced with the potential resentment and wrath of the person who is dying. There may be a fear of "saying the wrong thing", a kind of emotional helplessness spawned by the fear of failing as a carer. The immediate future is feared and the future beyond that may be unthinkably barren, devoid of all that the dying person means to us.

Restoring diminished energy

These fears, particularly if they are sustained over a long time, tend to drain your energy. You become listless, weary and your mental powers are affected. To help sustain yourself, you may find the suggestions for cultivating energy on pages 38–9 helpful as well as those for stress release on pages 88–91. In addition, you could try the Bach flower remedies which work on the level of the mind and emotions: Mimulus for everyday, named fears; Aspen for excessive fears, including the fear of death; Rock Rose for extreme panic. You may find the heart warming herbal infusion (page 84) useful, particularly if you feel you don't have the energy to deal with your fear.

Self-protection

When faced with great changes, the world we know appears to collapse around us. Our first reaction is often one of complete disbelief. "This is not possible." "I can't believe it." "This can't be happening to me." "There must have been some mistake." The worse the news, the less we want to hear it. Our control system refuses to allow us to hear it, let alone comprehend it. In many instances, people who are given a fatal diagnosis, simply do not take in what they are told – or subsequently act as if they had not been told.

We are all equipped with such natural self-protection mechanisms, which come into play automatically when we are injured or traumatized. What may appear from the outside to be an illogical or childish denial in the face of death may in fact be that person's way of instantly drawing a complete security cordon around themselves. This is their way of buying time in which to think about what to do next. In this way, their denial allows them to continue living even in the face of death. Depression, too, can serve this purpose of protective withdrawal and preservation.

Some people never emerge from that state. For some, the passion for life is too great for them to admit the reality of death. For others, the pain of losing everyone and everything they love is too much to face and their survival strategy is to avoid that heartbreak at all costs. For many, their denial is unconscious and automatic: the way they have lived up to that point has left them with no alternative behaviours to draw on.

Denial, anger and depression are often regarded as unhealthy responses to death. But an important distinction needs to be made between reactions which are part of a naturally evolving process of self-protection and those which are potentially harmful, both for oneself and others.

The power of anger

You may have been told that you or someone you love has a fatal illness. You may be seized by an anger unlike anything you have experienced. It may be so all-consuming that you cannot express it. This energy is extraordinarily powerful. People smash objects, shout and scream and endure intense pain without flinching.

*In the attempt
to defeat death
man has been
inevitably
obliged
to defeat life,
for the two are
inextricably
linked.*

HENRY MILLER

Whatever anger you feel is uniquely yours. For some people it is a kind of cosmic rage against the universe for permitting such suffering and injustice. Some feel it as a sharp, insistent grievance against someone specific – the driver of the car, the doctor at the hospital, even a close relation – who seems responsible for the tragedy.

The anger may crystallize like ice. You find yourself coldly observing the events around you in silence. Or you may erupt like fire, expressing yourself with obsessive intensity.

A startling quality of anger can be its insight. Far from being blinded, you may find yourself cutting through illusions and social niceties. This energy has the power to transform itself into illuminating wisdom. But if we remain completely overwhelmed and fixated, we risk destroying everything we hold dear.

The danger of collapse

Obstinately, we may refuse to admit that we are dying, or we may try every latest miracle cure, or we may lay accusations and curses at the doorstep of everyone we know and love – any or all of these can be our chosen exit script. But as events unfold, the psychic machinery of each of these strategies is liable to collapse without warning like a poorly erected scaffold. The result, more often than not, is depression. The depression of exhaustion, frustration and failure. Like an army which has run amok, we ourselves become the enemy we confront.

This is an age-old story. It is not the anger, the denial or the depression that is necessarily inappropriate. It is often our obstinacy and our fixation in these states that harms us most. Aggression, whether against ourselves or others, is ultimately self-defeating. The energy needed to sustain it burns out.

That recognition itself holds the seeds of precious insight. Like all breakdowns, it may also become our point of breakthrough.

Inner weather

Our reactions to death can become destructive. If denial, anger and depression become obsessive, the energy of hatred can explode outwards towards others or can strike inwardly where it manifests in self-destructive disorders, chief among them guilt.

Common reactions are to feel victimized by emotions, to suppress them or to act out their destructive fury. But like all energies, these forces also contain within them great potential. Their power may be exactly what you need to reconstruct your understanding and personal creativity in your greatest hour of need.

Getting in touch

Emotions are like our inner weather and it makes no more sense to suppress the facts about them, than to deny the existence of the daily weather forecast. The importance of acknowledging our emotions seems simple when stated, but many of us fear the strength of our feelings. Instead of learning to befriend, examine and live with our feelings, we have spent our lives doing the opposite.

Yet experience shows that it is when we refuse to acknowledge our emotions that they acquire the greatest power over us. When we are able to admit that we feel sad on one day and angry the next and are willing to share that fact straightforwardly with others, our emotions become life-size companions and a secret pain inside us is relieved.

If we refuse to acknowledge our emotions openly, the energy is often stored up as if in a reservoir, ready to be reactivated at another time. The repressed emotion will tend to express itself in distorted ways, at inappropriate times and towards the wrong targets. Or we may find ourselves acting out our unacknowledged emotions in uncontrollable ways: in our behaviour (being nasty to each other), in our body (developing stomach ulcers) or in our minds (experiencing pain with no physical cause).

Ingrained behaviours don't change all that easily. But death is the most powerful force for change that there is, and it offers us a clear choice that only we ourselves can make.

Happy and wise are those who endeavour to be during this life as they wish to be found at their death. Apply yourself so to live now, that at the hour of death, you may be glad and unafraid.

THOMAS À KEMPIS

IN THE MIRROR

One of the most distressing facts about the mood swings of dying people is that they often end up targeting those who care for them. A natural worry is that you might end up being hurtful like that yourself. Careful scrutiny of your behaviour in ordinary difficult situations may help you to recognize and address your own behaviour patterns.

Our destructive behaviour is often associated with deep feelings of fear and helplessness, and is a way of attempting to regain control or manifest our power. Do you see that in yourself?

We tend to regard the emotions of others differently from our own. People are commonly described as irrational, blind, prejudiced, selfish, hurtful and egotistical. What traces of these qualities do you see in any of your reactions?

Can you think of difficult situations where you were able to use your emotions to move forward in a constructive way? What have you learned from that?

How do you react when you are unable to control yourself and events around you?

How do you respond to the incompetence, insensitivity or aggression of the people you work or live with?

If events don't turn out the way you want them to, or people do things to which you object, do you feel the matter cannot be laid to rest until it is clear who is to blame?

If you are challenged with new information that conflicts with your ideas, what do you feel about changing your viewpoint?

How do you react if someone accuses you of being "emotional"?

What do you find it easiest to forgive? What have you never been able to forgive?

Restoring balance

The very essence of life is change, while the essence of clinging is to retain, to stabilize, to prevent change. That is why change appears to us as suffering. If we did not regard objects or states of existence from the standpoint of possession or selfish enjoyment, we should not feel in the least troubled by their change or even by their disappearance. It is therefore not the "world" or its transitions which is the cause of suffering but our attitude towards it, our clinging, our thirst, our ignorance.

LAMA GOVINDA

The forces of a tornado twist violently like a gigantic spinning top, creating a distinctive dark funnel sweeping across the horizon. At the heart of the column, however, the countervailing energies render the eye of the storm calm and undisturbed.

This peace is not the absence of conflict. It is the balance of forces.

Each of us has this same capacity to find balance in the midst of powerful forces. That ability emerges in us, not as a mysterious other-worldly spirit, but as we go deeper and deeper into the fullness of our own human experience.

We constantly seek this balance of forces. We do it in our own ways – often in ways not understood by others. As long as we live, we are engaged in this perpetual balancing and rebalancing. It lies at the heart of everything we experience as we die.

That experience is deeply personal and expresses itself uniquely in each individual. It is therefore thought sometimes that the quest for balance, or for harmony as the sages of ancient China would call it, is a solitary venture.

But the energies we seek to balance are also part of our common humanity, and of our participation in the larger energies around us. We can use their power not only to help ourselves and each other as we live, but also as we die.

The ancient Taoist symbol of Yin/Yang. At the fullest point of the light, a dark circle signals the emergence of night; in the depth of the night, a light circle represents the coming of day. Inner harmony is achieved by perceiving this perpetual interchange in all things. It is known as the Way of Nature.

Learning the lesson

The transformations we experience are endless. We go through many births after we are born. We die many deaths before we die. For many people it is these countless changes and losses that evoke the greatest fear and cause the greatest suffering. For so many of us, it is the actual process of transformation we fear, far more than death.

Inexhaustible wisdom is inherent in what we fear. Our bodies are perpetually giving way and being reconstructed; we experience sickness and injury throughout life. We ignore these messengers of death, regain a measure of health and carry on. We fail to see how everything in our minds, our bodies and in front of our eyes arises and passes away, disappears and returns.

Then, as if we had failed to learn our lesson, our bodies finally instruct us fully in our mortality.

Whenever we are ready to open our hearts fully to that lesson, a larger reality is revealed beyond the strategies we have developed for our temporary survival.

We are then ready to receive the wisdom of the words of the Abbé Abraham à Santa Clara when he wrote: "A man who dies before he dies does not die when he dies."

IN THE MIRROR

Although we are constantly being reminded of death, we tend to put it out of our minds. Thus, when we are confronted with major illness and disability, we are all too often completely unprepared for it, mentally, emotionally and physically. You can ask yourself:

Are you already overwhelmed by the petty problems and inconveniences of daily life? How do you experience them? Are they ever seen as reminders of the fleeting fragility of life?

How do you respond when you are ill or have an injury? Are you angry, depressed or resentful? Are these the feelings you wish to have while dying?

What is your reaction when other people have accidents, fall ill or die? What have you learned about yourself from these events and your reactions to them? What do you think you have left to learn?

Intimacy

Death itself is not a communicable disease. The fear of death is. If we treat a person with a terminal illness as if they are in quarantine, that is exactly what we are communicating. In fact, very few conditions automatically preclude the person from being touched, hugged, kissed, slept with or made love to, if that is what is wanted by those involved.

A common fear is that sex may kill the person who is dying. But the medical evidence is that fewer than one per cent of patients with severe heart troubles die directly as a result of the excitement caused by sex. On the other hand, it is part of popular mythology that dying during orgasm is a sublime experience. In fact, some people with a terminal diagnosis exhibit an intense burst of sexual frenzy. Some observers dismiss this as merely a refusal to die. But it may stem from an intensified love of life, a pleasurable release from pain, and a renewed longing for the other person.

A person may become so obsessed with their condition that they lose interest in anything or anyone else. Some conditions and medication may reduce a person's sex drive; if they and their lover are not alerted to this, both may suffer in embarrassed silence and pull apart. Some forms of disfigurement can also prove to be insuperable obstacles.

Maintaining contact and intimacy depends on the courage to be open with one's lover and to express deep feelings. The pain of making that effort is ultimately more productive than the pain of not trying.

If you are a distant relative or friend visiting an elderly person, the impact of your touch may be greatly amplified by the simple fact that the person may have lived for years without any physical human contact.

We are put on earth a little space
That we may learn to bear the beams of love.

WILLIAM BLAKE

Human contact

Intimacy may be so associated with sex that it makes it difficult
for some people to touch others or to accept being touched.
However, touching someone is also part of healing and
comforting. It is part of our natural response to human suffering.
Touching, even if awkward, is part of the rich language of
human contact. Our sense of touch is one of the first to develop
and one of the last to go. Resting your hand on the person's
forearm, holding their hand or giving them a massage are all
ways of being present and fully with them.

Touching meets another instinctive need. Communication
studies show that we take in most of what another person
conveys from their non-verbal gestures rather than the words
they use. Touch is therefore one of the single most powerful
means of communication we have. If you have no idea what to
say to another person, extend your hand to them and make
contact; that alone is a far more eloquent statement than almost
anything you could say.

IN THE MIRROR

If you have been unable to express or accept intimacy in your life, it is
expecting a lot to think that the encounter with death will automatically
change this. On the other hand, sometimes it is exactly a shock of that
magnitude that can break us out of our ingrained patterns.

*Are you someone who is able to be intimate with others and to touch them when
that is an appropriate expression of deep feeling?*

*Do you react with hesitation if someone touches you, particularly in periods of
stress, or do you appreciate their warmth and reciprocate?*

*As you reflect on your own death or the death of someone you are close to, is
there any behaviour which you would like to adopt as an authentic expression of
your inner feelings?*

Engagement

William Blake died painting, Mozart died composing, St Francis died singing. Some people die working, some listening to music, some making love, some in deep meditation.

Many people die the way they have lived and wish to be helped to do that right up to their final moments. Whether this is possible depends, naturally, on the nature of their illness; but even here the human spirit can manifest extraordinary powers. As we come to understand more about the potential of the end of life, more and more carers are opening up possibilities for people to express their creativity, despite their illness.

For some people it is very clear what they wish to do. All they need is to be provided with the facilities. For example, they may need to have a frame to help them continue oil painting, or writing or reading while bedbound. If they are working on a project, they may need to use the home computer or to have someone read to them, take dictation or transcribe tapes.

Exploring inner potential

Other people appreciate some initial help in getting started. They feel they would like to express themselves in some way, but have no previous experience. Those who work with the dying are learning to encourage people to explore their potential. One way is to focus on the person's immediate experience: their illness and death. The carer or counsellor may ask spontaneous questions to open up the subject. How would the person like to be remembered? How would they like their funeral to be conducted? What has been important in their lives?

If the person has no children, they may feel they are leaving nothing behind. Is there anything they would like to begin now and then leave behind? Some people want to plant the seeds for future shrubs and trees. Some are inspired to try their hand at painting or making music – or learning to appreciate these arts. One mother started a personal book of humour and asked each visitor to write their favourite jokes in it, thereby creating a unique, collective memorial.

Turn up the lights; I don't want to go home in the dark.

LAST WORDS
OF O. HENRY

Personal statements

It can be a deeply moving experience to work with a person who is exploring what they want out of preparing to die. For some people it is like a pilgrimage, in which their own lives are both the journey and the journey's end. As they experience the power of what they are going through, they may feel they are losing their senses or their rationality. They need someone to be with them to affirm the importance of what they are going through and to support them.

If you are helping someone in this way, it may be important for you to focus your attention on the significance of the various symbols or reminiscences to which the person is particularly attached. Why are certain things important, why certain places, certain people, or certain colours? What do they symbolize for that person?

Some people are using video cameras to record messages or testimonials which they can leave to their families, lovers, spouse and children. Making such a personal statement can be extremely powerful for the person, the people helping them and for all those who receive it. Intense emotion may be released. At moments there can be considerable pain, but the rewards for all involved can be enormous. "You'll all cry", says one professional using such methods, "but this is where the boundaries dissolve, when they understand that you are with them in your full humanity."

The Internet opens up possibilities for contact with people around the world and access to vast sources of information, entertainment and inspiration. Providing this facility to a dying person and their carers is increasingly feasible and the home computer can be easily adjusted for operation even from a bed. It can literally keep a person plugged into global consciousness and able to interact with it whenever they wish.

The movement of energy

What we call dying is the dispersal of the body's energies. This dissolution is described in many different ways around the world. Whether you view the process from a scientific or religious point of view, there is a fundamental pattern. The essential life force which manifests in all the body's cells, in all the life processes of the body and in the activity of the brain and nervous system begins to decline. The energy is weaker, it moves more sluggishly and it is unable to reach all parts of the body. As its power ebbs, it loses its ability to hold the system together and to sustain the myriad internal chemical and electrical interactions that keep us functioning.

Each human death is like the death of a galaxy. If we could be placed under a vast electron microscope, that is exactly what we would look like and, as we died, we would witness some parts of the galaxy collapsing, others exploding, some spinning apparently beyond control, some slowing down and freezing over. And as one stream of energy in the system underwent these changes, it would trigger off corresponding transformations elsewhere in the inner dynamics of the galaxy.

The sum total of the energy is not lost, but it ceases to operate according to the complex pattern to which we have become accustomed. It is like the untying of a knot. The rope remains, but the knot is no longer apparent.

The elements

This process of dispersal is described in several Asian medical systems as the dissipation of the specific energies that comprise human beings. They may speak of the disintegration of the Earth element (as our body begins to lose strength). Then follows the dissolution of the Water element (as the bodily fluids are no longer regulated), then the dissipation of the Fire element (as we lose heat and our mind swings between confusion and clarity), and finally the dispersal of the Air element (as we begin to breathe our last and have visions).

The energy model

Contemporary scientific investigations and religious thought tend increasingly to agree on a fundamental life force in the universe. Many terms are used, all aiming to describe our awareness of the energy that imbues every aspect of our experience. This perception makes us look on matters of life and death with fresh eyes (see page opposite).

Dying in a changing universe

How does death fit into the equation $E=MC^2$? Our conventional assumptions about existence, space and time have been called into question by Einstein's theory of relativity. We now know that our universe is a vast field of energy and that everything we experience, including ourselves, emerges out of that field and returns to it. The most recent discoveries of sub-atomic physics are even more profound. The notion of anything – or anyone – having a finite existence, either in time or space, is a temporary perception. What we experience are endlessly changing patterns of energy.

These scientific findings appear to fly in the face of common sense, but just as the heretical discoveries of Galileo ultimately revealed to us a cosmos of inestimable splendour, so the universe being examined by quantum physicists now invites us to see our lives in a wholly new dimension.

As fields of vibrating energy, we are constantly engaged in an interchange with the rest of the entire cosmos. We resemble standing wave patterns, perpetually changing and being re-created. The energetic matter of which we exist at any one moment is exchanged for other wave-like particles in the next. Not only are we interconnected with each other and all that exists, we are each other. And everything that exists or has ever existed is, at some point, us.

So where does that leave our idea of death? And where does it leave the barriers we think we have erected between each other?

Reaching out

Many of the barriers we face in life are ones we have somehow made for ourselves. Many of our reactions to death show this in the starkest possible light. But precisely because they are self-created, we have it within our power to see through them and reach out beyond them if we wish. The combination of social taboo, the medicalization of death and our own ignorance inhibit us from accepting and giving some of the most valuable care and support possible at the time of death – despite the fact that methods for doing this have been handed down from ancient times.

A common feature of many traditional and complementary healing systems is their ability to understand and work with the energy of the human body, in times of both health and illness. Their wisdom often involves direct contact between people at a deep human level, including those who are dying and those caring for them.

The specific techniques introduced in this book derive from that tradition but are not demanding. Therapeutic contact helps you support the person, but is not draining in the same way that prolonged conversation can be. The work is mutual, because both people give and receive. Furthermore, as explained on pages 36–7, even at fairly advanced stages of illness the dying person can reciprocate if they wish. This can be immensely rewarding and a wonderful expression of love.

Your response

These trigger questions may help you assess your own openness to this approach on a personal level:

Would you be resistant to receiving physiotherapy or massage for an injury? Would you have the same reaction if it could help relieve the pain of a terminal illness?

If you knew that applying proven techniques of relaxation therapy, such as hand and foot massage, or herbal extracts could greatly ease the transition from life to death of someone you love, is there any reason why you would not be willing to experiment with that?

To die is to go into the Collective Unconscious, to lose oneself in order to be transformed into form, pure form.

HERMANN HESSE

Death with dignity

Doctors often argue that "death with dignity" is a fantasy that simply does not fit the facts. "Dying is a series of destructive events that involve by their very nature the disintegration of the dying person's humanity," would be a typical expression of this point of view. The intention behind such remarks is often deep compassion – to prevent individuals and their relatives pinning their hopes on an idealized "happy death" – and thereby setting themselves up for feeling guilty, angry and vengeful when the physical decay of the body sets in.

Studies of patients' final moments, however, do not suggest that our humanity is necessarily destroyed. A survey of over 35,000 observations by doctors and nurses, conducted by Karlis Osis, found that 10 per cent of patients appeared conscious in the hour before death, that fear was not dominant and that one in twenty showed signs of elation.

"I have done years of nursing, often with terminal patients, and have seen many deaths," Fiona Ann Monsell told the Institute for Social Inventions in London. "I have never seen anyone die in panic. Quite often patients will rally around within three days of death to say goodbye to their loved ones, some have said they've seen relatives that have gone before them, but at the end none has ever been afraid.

"When my mother died, some 15 months ago, I was at her bedside and held her hand, and the moment she passed on I felt her leaving and pass through me on her way. I can only describe it as a beautiful experience that I shall never forget. It was like she gave me a small part of her energy to keep with me always."

PART FOUR

Giving and letting go

GROWING

•

FORGIVING

•

PREPARING TO DIE

May your eyes mingle with the sun.
May your breath be merged with the winds.
May the waters of your being mingle with the oceans.
May the ashes become one with the soil.
May you go to the heavens or to the earth,
whatever your direction may be.

THE VEDAS

Completing your work

In *The Book of the Dead* of Ancient Egypt, the souls of the dead were weighed on the pans of a vast scale to determine their fate in the afterlife. If their hearts weighed as little as a feather, the symbol of truth, the dead spirit was led to a life of eternal happiness in the Kingdom of Osiris.

It is a haunting image, evoking the deep emotional need that so many people feel to empty their hearts and speak freely before death. This is not necessarily the same as settling old scores or totalling up all the accounts of your lifetime. Indeed, if you manage to live fully up to your death, there will always be some business not yet completed.

Nevertheless, when it becomes clear that you have a condition from which you may not recover, you are being given an unmistakable signal that it is time to reconsider the priorities in your life. Doing this may become more important to you than anything else and override all other concerns, possibly even pressures to undergo intensive, enervating medical treatments.

Time for communication

You may have fresh, intense feelings about those people to whom you are closest. Are there important obligations to them that you want to fulfil if you can? Are there important conversations that you want to have with them? Are there messages that you want to convey to people whom you no longer see, but feel strongly about? Is there anything you want to give to, or share with, any of these people? Is there any misunderstanding or hard feeling that you wish to clear up?

Your own needs

You may have postponed doing things that need to be done and which have a particular resonance for you. Is there something you feel a deep need to complete, more than anything else? Is there something you wish to write down or record in some way about your life? Do you have a debt to another person or to an institution that you have always wanted to repay in some fitting way? Is there somewhere you have dreamed of visiting or something that you have wanted to do if you had the chance?

*I fall
and burst
beneath
the sacred
human tree.*

*Release
my seed and
let me fall.*

MURIEL LE SUEUR

Closing the circle

You may find that you are seized with innumerable regrets, suddenly feeling that you have not done any of the things you wanted to in life. These are the ghosts of old dreams that now risk dragging you backwards into your past. The challenge before you is to draw on the sum total of your life experience and listen to the inner voice which tells you what it is you most want to do *now* and what it is that will close the natural circle of your life.

IN THE MIRROR

If it helps us to breathe more freely having dealt with unfinished business at the time of death, you might ask yourself "What am I waiting for?" You may be someone who has months left to live, or years. Why accumulate deep regrets, unexpressed feelings and unexplored ambitions while you are living, only to carry them around like excess baggage until the last moments of your life?

If we are not open to loving and caring now, how can we expect suddenly to accept it in the midst of extreme fear, confusion and pain? If we cling to a selfish view of life, why should we expect to be generous in death? Looked at the other way round, if the sheer power of death offers such capacity for transformation, how can we tap into it now?

A common exercise in helping people prepare for death is to ask them to list what they would do if they had ten years, five years, six months and then finally one month to live. This helps them confront the reality of their eventual death. Often there is something that keeps reappearing in the different lists and the person is urged to reflect on the importance this has for them.

You could think about using exactly this same exercise to help you kick-start the rest of your life. Your list of things to do in the month before you die could become your agenda for the next month you live.

Social pressures

Even in the most mundane matters, your existence continues after your last breath. Responsibility for dealing with your body passes to your next of kin or appointed representative. But if you want to leave behind an atmosphere of genuine support for your loved ones, be clear *in advance* about what is likely to happen and what your wishes are.

Official procedures

Whether you die in a hospital, in a hospice or at home, your death must be registered. In the event of an unexpected or accidental death, an autopsy may be required by law. In some places, the police may investigate a natural home death, even when it is attended by a doctor. There will be forms to complete, offices to visit and officials to meet. It is a wise idea to think about who in the family is going to deal with this and have them find out what is involved (see "Your Death File", right).

Funeral arrangements

The pressure from undertakers or funeral directors on your relations and loved ones can be intense. In the midst of their grief, they may find themselves made to feel guilty if they do not give you a conventional – and expensive – funeral. Many families resent this. Others find themselves deeply divided on the issue. The only real defence is being clear about your wishes in advance, in writing, and in consultation with those who will handle your funeral arrangements (see pages 136–7)

The cost need not be high

Over fourteen billion dollars a year are spent on funerals in the United States alone. Even burial in an unmarked, communal grave can cost several thousand dollars. In the United Kingdom, an average commercial funeral is estimated to be over a thousand pounds. But the fact is that you can purchase a professional body bag or a biodegradable coffin and independently rent crematorium facilities for a tenth of that cost. The best advice is to examine the alternatives and be clear about what you want.

Your Death File

A simple gesture that you can make to your family to ease matters for them after your death is to create a file with all the information they will need about you in the event of your death. Make sure you regularly update it.

Your file should contain:

birth certificate

details of passport (you might die abroad)

your will

your Living Will (Advance Directive)

an enduring power of attorney

your organ donor approval

details of your bank account, credit cards

investments and other details

insurance policies

pre-paid or other funeral plans

people you want notified, including employers

any specific requests or wishes not in your will

You can maintain the file lovingly since you are doing this for the people you care most about, and you can leave any messages there for them to support them if you die without warning.

To be seen as I am, preparing for death by thinking about it and making funeral and burial arrangements, is often considered a morbid obsession by some friends and family. I am forced to do these things quietly and secretively because they are thought to be negative and unhelpful. But why should I have to abandon reason in matters of death? Shouldn't we all be concerned with this, the only certainty in life?

BARBARA RAE

Attitudes

Other people's attitudes towards death can have a powerful and often disturbing effect on those who live on after you. You cannot anticipate everything, but it is enormously helpful to encourage your loved ones to imagine what they might encounter and discuss that with them. That way, they can have the memory of your thoughts and feelings to guide them – and the discussion may prove to be immensely helpful to you as well.

Sometimes surviving relatives face these difficulties from those around them:

Cultural and community pressures to conduct the funeral or rites of mourning in ways that go against the wishes of the dead person or family.

Pressures from other family members who insist that they know best how the dead person should be treated, even if that is not what the deceased wanted.

Religious or psychological advice that implies that relatives should feel a certain way or hold certain beliefs, or moral sentiments that imply that there is something wrong with the way relatives (or the deceased) have acted.

Social avoidance such as acquaintances crossing to the other side of the street rather than talking to the bereaved.

Intrusive caring from people who think they know what is best for people in grief, rather than simply being present, open-hearted and unconditional.

Making up your mind

I am a temporary enclosure for a temporary purpose;
that served, my skull and teeth, my idiosyncrasy
and desire, will disperse, I believe, like the timbers
of a booth after the fair.

H.G. WELLS

One of the apparent paradoxes of dying well is that it requires the will power to let go. You need to decide about how you wish to be treated – and you must make those decisions while you are capable of doing so. Most people agree with this idea, but they actually put off any decision-making. In effect, they allow themselves to abandon their own autonomy.

The consequences are serious. Most people die without a will. That places a terrible burden on the surviving family members or partner. If there is no legally binding record of the person's wishes, it is left to their loved ones to decide what to do. If there has been no discussion with the dying person, as is often the case, then deeply wounding arguments can ensue about the funeral, the disposal of the body and the distribution of any property that may be left behind. And, in many cases, if there is no will, significant sums may be consumed unnecessarily in taxes and professional fees. Making a will, no matter how simple, also helps to anchor your current thoughts about the reality of your death, and it can be amended at any time if you wish to make changes.

One of the most basic acts of generosity and gratitude towards those you love is to complete a will at the earliest possible opportunity.

The gift of life

We don't like to admit it, but we live in a world where accidents can happen to us at any time. "The life of beings is like a bubble", says an ancient text. If you are killed, it is increasingly common for doctors to seek to use your vital organs for transplants that will help another person live, restore their sight or end the misery of artificial life support systems. Don't leave the burden of that decision to your shocked loved ones. Decide now, put it in your will and, if you wish, register as an organ donor.

Decisions and responsibilities

The following checklist gathers together the essential questions that are presented at various points throughout this book. If you have responsibility for a dying person, you should review these points with them so that you are clear about their wishes. If you are well and healthy, now is a good time to ask yourself these questions, too. Bear in mind that circumstances may not always make it possible for all your wishes to be met.

Places

How important to you is the environment in which you will die?

Do you have preferences about dying in a hospital, a hospice, at home or in a nursing home?

People

Are there people you would like to see and spend time with?

Are there issues you want to sort out with specific individuals?

Are there any people you don't want to have around? Why?

Treatment

What information do you expect to be told about your illness and the options for treatment?

Is there any form of treatment you do not want to have under any circumstances?

Have you made your wishes clear in a Living Will? (see pages 136–7)

Attitude

What sort of attitude would you like other people to have towards you when you are dying?

Is there anything you would like specially provided at that time?

Are there any spiritual or religious practices that you wish to be observed?

Is there anything that you don't want people to do for you?

After death

Is there any spiritual or religious practice you wish carried out at the time of death or immediately afterwards?

Is there anything you wish done for those you love?

What funeral or memorial arrangements would you like made?

Have you made a will? (see pages 134–5)

Giving

*I would like to believe that when I die I have given myself away
like a tree that sows seed every spring and never counts the loss,
because it is not loss, it is adding to future life. It is the tree's way of
being. Strongly rooted perhaps, but spilling out its treasure on the wind.*

MAY SARTON

Death naturally opens the door to generosity of
spirit. None of your possessions will belong to you
after your death, but they may be cherished by others
because they were yours when you were alive. In
this way, when you bequeath what you own, you are
giving to others an enduring part of your life.

This is also an opportunity to reflect on what, in
a deeper sense, any of us can truly say is ours. You
may come to see everything you have acquired as
human artefacts held by you in trust. As you pass
them on to others, you are fulfilling the responsibility
of that trust.

Your reflections may lead you to express your
generosity while you are still living, giving the
people or institutions in your life those things and
resources that you want them to have. There is no
need to wait until after your death.

Your carers

Another gift you can give is to reciprocate the
attention of your carers. They too need support and
human warmth. Depending on your condition, you
can encourage them to take care of themselves by
following the relaxation and other exercises in this
book. You can do the exercises with them or help
guide them. You can also learn the techniques for
hand massage and regularly give them the benefit of
your touch. This does not require much energy and
you may be able to give in this way until shortly
before your death. You will be truly following the
old maxim: "When you give, give of yourself."

Your body

Depending on your physical condition, you can
consider donating your body to medical science. This
can be a priceless gift and one you should discuss
with your doctor and next of kin. You could enable
another person to live after you or contribute to their
learning so that they can care for others.

Your Will

Everyone has the right to make a will. In many countries, this is normally done with the specialist help of a lawyer – and if you have complicated financial affairs, it is best to do this. But you also have the option of simply discussing your wishes with your closest relatives and drawing up a basic will, stating what is to be done after your death and who will be responsible for handling your affairs (known as the "executor"). You do not need a special form, but if you wish, you can normally obtain a will form in any stationers. Organizations that support dying people can also advise in case there are formalities that you need to follow in the jurisdiction where you live (see Resources, pages 184–7). Otherwise, you can simply use the following formula:

THE WILL OF

NAME ....

ADDRESS ....

I revoke all previous wills and codicils and I appoint to be my executor:

1. NAME ....

    ADDRESS ....

2. I give ....

    ....

    ....

    ....

    ....

    ....

    ....

    ....

    ....

3. YOUR SIGNATURE ....

4. Signed by the testator in our presence, and then by us in his or her presence

    on the   day of   in the year

    WITNESS SIGNATURE ....

    NAME ....

    ADDRESS ....

    OCCUPATION ....

    WITNESS SIGNATURE ....

    NAME ....

    ADDRESS ....

    OCCUPATION ....

1. *Insert the full name and full address of the person(s) you wish to handle your legal affairs after your death (such as your spouse, partner or next of kin).*

2. *Indicate whatever you wish to give and to whom. If you want to leave everything to the person who is your executor, all you need say is:* everything to my executor. *You can also specify any requests about your funeral or other arrangements you want made after your death.*

3. *Then sign your will, watched by two witnesses of legal age, neither of whom is an executor or beneficiary. Sign immediately under the statement of your wishes, leaving no space.*

4. *Have each witness sign and date the will. Below each signature have them print their full name, address and occupation.*

Keep one copy of your will in your Death File (see page 130) and give one to your executor.

Your Living Will

One of the great ironies of medical science is that, in the fight against disease and death, people can end up being treated with the best of intentions but with technology that actually prolongs their suffering. Many people and their relatives or partners believe the suffering is worth it and request medical staff to do everything possible for their loved ones. Increasingly, however, more and more people are taking steps to reclaim a measure of control over the final stages of their lives.

One such step is the Living Will. This is also known as an Advance Directive. In the same way that a normal will specifies your wishes after your death, a Living Will sets out your wishes about how you want to be treated if you are dying and unable to participate in decision-making.

Living Wills do not endorse or request euthanasia or mercy killing. They are accepted by numerous regulatory bodies of the medical profession. Legislation upholding Living Wills is now widespread throughout the United States and court judgments in other countries, including the United Kingdom, are beginning to uphold them as well.

A Living Will serves several purposes. It speaks for you when you cannot, guiding the most difficult decisions that your loved ones and doctors have to make. This ensures respect for your integrity, individuality and autonomy, even if you are unconscious. It also provides authenticated documentation of your wishes about the withholding or withdrawal of life-sustaining treatment.

A practical step

Making a Living Will confers powerful immediate benefits. It is a constructive way of focusing your mind on your own death and how you wish to be treated. For example, if you were completely paralysed in a car crash and could no longer breathe on your own, would you wish to have your life prolonged indefinitely by artificial ventilation?

Your Living Will is definitely something about which you should consult your nearest relations or loved ones. This helps to ensure that they understand your real intentions and offers a practical basis for a frank and loving discussion about dealing with each other's deaths.

Making your Living Will

1
Obtain a Living Will form or use the model (right).
2
Complete it, adding or deleting any points you wish.
3
Discuss it with your nearest relations or loved ones.
4
Discuss it with your doctor.
5
Complete it, sign it and have it witnessed.
6
Deposit a copy in your Death File and with your lawyer or executor and doctor.
7
Review it from time to time and make any changes you wish in line with your evolving views.
8
See Resources (pages 184–7) for organizations that can advise you.

Model Living Will

TO ALL HEALTH CARE PROFESSIONALS, FRIENDS AND OTHER PEOPLE CONCERNED, this Advance Directive is made by me at a time when I am of sound mind and after careful consideration.

I wish to be fully informed about any illness I may have. This is to include informing me about alternative treatments that are available and whatever risks and possible outcomes that need to be taken into account in any decision-making regarding those treatments and my future at that point.

I DECLARE that if at any time the following circumstances exist, namely:

a) I suffer from one or more of the conditions in the Schedule of Conditions; and
b) I have become unable to participate effectively in decisions about my medical care; and
c) two independent physicians (one a consultant) are of the opinion that I am unlikely to recover from illness or impairment involving severe distress;

Then and in those circumstances my directions are as follows:

1. that I am not to be subjected to any medical intervention or treatment aimed at prolonging or sustaining my life, subject to the considerations in Point 4 below;
2. that any distressing symptoms (including any caused by lack of food) are to be fully controlled by appropriate analgesic or other treatment, even though that treatment may shorten my life;
3. that I am not to be forcibly fed (although I may be given water to drink);
4. that any of my organs which can be transplanted to other people who are in need of them be removed while they are in suitable condition for transplantation.

I CONSENT to anything proposed to be done or omitted in compliance with the directions expressed above and absolve my medical attendants from any civil liability arising out of such acts or omissions.

I WISH to be as conscious as my circumstances permit (allowing for adequate pain control) as death approaches. I ask my medical attendants to bear this statement in mind when considering what my intentions would be in any uncertain situation.

IN THE EVENT of any uncertainty as to my wishes and my inability for any reason to be able to participate effectively in decisions about my medical care, all decisions regarding my treatment, pain control, and the cessation of life support in any form may be taken by the person to whom I have assigned Enduring Power of Attorney.

I RESERVE the right to revoke this Advance Directive at any time, but unless I do so it should be taken to represent my continuing directions.

SCHEDULE OF CONDITIONS
1. Advance disseminated malignant disease
2. Severe immune deficiency
3. Advanced degenerative disease of the nervous system
4. Severe and lasting brain damage due to injury, stroke, disease or other cause
5. Senile or pre-senile dementia, whether Alzheimer's, multi-infarct or other
6. Any other condition of comparable gravity

I HAVE LODGED a copy of this Living Will with the following doctor:

NAME ....

ADDRESS ....

TELEPHONE NUMBER ....

Should I become unable to communicate my wishes as stated above and should amplification be required, I have appointed the following person to represent these wishes on my behalf and I want this person to be consulted by those caring for me and/or this person's representation of my views to be respected as it is to them that I have assigned Enduring Power of Attorney:

NAME ....

ADDRESS ....

TELEPHONE NUMBER ....

YOUR SIGNATURE ....

DATE ....

NAME ....

ADDRESS: ....

WE TESTIFY that the above-named signed this Advance Directive in our presence, and made it clear to us that he understood what it meant. We do not know of any pressure being brought on him to make such a directive and we believe it was made by his own wish. We are over 18, we are not relatives of the above-named, nor do we stand to gain from his death.

WITNESS SIGNATURE ....

NAME ....

ADDRESS ....

WITNESS SIGNATURE ....

NAME ....

ADDRESS ....

A legacy for others

What you give to others is not merely what you possess; what you leave behind is not solely what you have accomplished. At every moment of your life and in the period of your death, you shape the future of others. You do this in many ways, but the most powerful and the most pervasive is the impact that you make upon other people's understanding of themselves and their underlying attitudes towards life. One of the greatest legacies you can leave them is the impact of your own preparation for death, your own understanding of it and the manner of your dying.

The great theologian, Abbé de Tocqville, observed: "I have seen many people die. None were afraid when it was close up." Unfortunately, many people are not encouraged to share with others their changing perceptions as they face death. Yet those insights can be of great value and should not be dismissed as merely the random reflections of a sick person.

Passing on prejudice

The fears and other assumptions we have about death, like so many other attitudes, are often the accumulated and unquestioned prejudices we have absorbed from others while growing up. These remain in place while the world around us changes and while we ourselves change. The ideas may have been valid at one time, but they may no longer be helpful to us in the present. We suddenly discover this when we face a crisis or threat. If the sediment of inherited ideas remains in our memory unexamined, we find ourselves merely reverting to phrases or social attitudes ingrained in us as children. In effect, we tend to pass on to others what we were told ourselves decades earlier. It is as if we had bypassed our own life's experience.

Death is the supreme festival on the road to freedom.

DIETRICH
BONHOEFFER

Making use of your life

One potentially useful exercise that you can experiment with is to list the attitudes about death you picked up early in your life. Then think about the attitudes you now have. They may have remained the same or may have changed. This gives you an opportunity to examine the reasons for the attitudes you now have and the experiences that have led you to your conclusions.

You might be someone who has not thought about this at all, in which case this exercise could be immensely beneficial – it can help to clarify a great deal of what you have been through and what you are now going through.

This is an exercise that can be done either by an individual privately, or involving loved ones and family. There are no right or wrong answers. Indeed, many people might have to admit that they are rather confused about their answers – and everyone's answers can change over time. In any discussion, it is most helpful to concentrate on listening and understanding what everyone is saying, rather than contradicting or proposing alternative intellectual theories. What matters most is speaking from the heart – and listening.

For each question ask yourself: "What was I told earlier in my life?" and then "What would I like to pass on as my legacy?"

Question	What I was told	My legacy
1. *What is the effect of thinking about death?*	morbid & abnormal	healthy & constructive
2. *How should we deal with our feelings about death?*		
3. *What is the greatest help to a dying person?*		
4. *What is the greatest help to those who love and care for a dying person?*		
5. *What spiritual care do we need?*		
6. *What should happen at a funeral?*		
7. *How do we dispose of our possessions?*		

Keep growing

From the time of being diagnosed with a potentially life-threatening illness, what use are we to make of the days, months and years left to us? We are losing our old selves, losing a body which no longer works as it used to, losing our future. The vivid and unfinished dramas of our lifetime pass chaotically before the mind. We turn inward.

Our silence is our chrysalis. Within it we protect ourselves like a wounded animal. Yet within that same space, the mind is preparing itself for a new reality.

Understanding this process puts death in a different context. On what inner work will we be engaged in the depths of our chrysalis?

First comes self-acceptance. This is what happens in the obsessive life review, repeated again and again until finally we cease trying to be anyone other than ourselves.

To the extent that we achieve that, progressively more energy is released so that we expand beyond the confines of our old self. This is when so many people begin to demonstrate fresh generosity of spirit, healing old rifts, thinking of others in need and giving of themselves.

For many, this broadening out accompanies awakened interest in religion, their own spirituality or their search for meaning. It may also be a period of quietude or of deep absorption in the wonders of nature.

Yet, however much we yearn for peace at the end of our days, it may only come to us in fitful moments between exhausting treatments and debilitating symptoms. Hence the supreme importance attached by so many traditions to the preparation for death and the careful practice of the ways by which the mind can be guided through it.

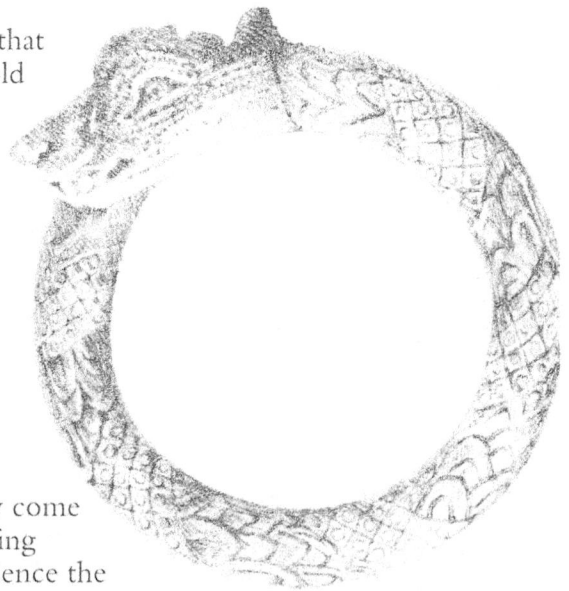

This African snake bracelet symbolizes life, continuity and eternity. Just as a snake sheds its skin and emerges afresh, much traditional wisdom understands human death as a spiritual transformation which occurs as we shed the worn out skin of this lifetime.

The waterfall

Our journey is like a mighty waterfall, said Zen Master Shunryu Suzuki Roshi. At the top of the waterfall and the bottom, there is the river. It is the same river, the same water. But as the river cascades over the edge and downwards, it does not fall as a single body of water. It separates into countless streams and tiny droplets. Transformed into separate currents, there is great turbulence. The water seems to boil and there is the constant roaring sound of the waterfall. It is as if the water can no longer move effortlessly when it is broken apart and it experiences confusion and turmoil as it falls.

In the same way, said the master, before birth and after death we are like the water of the flowing river. It is only after birth that we experience this sense of separateness, of difficulty and all our feelings. Not realizing that we are still one with the river, we have great fear.

But at the bottom of the waterfall, at the end of its journey, the turbulent water returns to its original oneness with the river and continues its inexorable movement to the sea.

"How very glad the water must be to return to the original river," he said. *"If this is so, what feeling will we have when we die? We will have perfect composure then, perfect composure."*

Lord, grant that my last hour may be my best hour.

OLD ENGLISH PRAYER

Forgiveness

This is time for the removal of all barriers. The barriers between ourselves and others, the barriers between our own mind and the inner depths of our being. The barriers which create anxiety and tension, mistrust and uncertainty, divisiveness and resentment.

The text on these pages can be used to guide your thoughts in private, or can be read aloud by friends or partners to each other. This healing practice can be shared at any time and is by no means reserved for those who are ill.

You may prefer to use another text on love, mercy and forgiveness. Simply read slowly, allowing time between the sentences for silence and acceptance.

~

While you are sitting or lying still, let your mind come to rest.

Feel the weight of your body coming to rest. Your hands resting. Your feet resting. Your whole body letting all its weight simply rest and be still. Rest fully in yourself.

Let your wandering mind rest gently on your breath.

Rest on your breath as it enters and departs.

Each breath, as it enters, is welcomed like a guest. As each breath leaves, the body relaxes and is grateful.

Feel the fullness of each breath as it enters and descends into you. Feel the muscles of your belly as they receive each breath. Then feel your body giving up the breath, releasing it. This is the deepest movement of the breath.

Rest your mind on the depth of that movement, as the breath fills your body and departs. Make room for the breath. Let the depths of your body soften. Be spacious – breathe in. Be at ease – release the breath.

There is space between each breath. Rest there, in that space. Be spacious in yourself.

In the depths of your being, turn gently towards yourself.

See your restlessness and come to rest. Rest in yourself kindly and with great care. Take rest in yourself.

Silently, in the soft depths of your being, repeat these ancient words: *"May I be free from suffering. May I be at peace."*

Let these words ride the rising and falling of your breath. Breathe in: *"May I be free from suffering."* Breathe out: *"May I be at peace."*

Let peace be restored with these words. *"May I be free from suffering. May I be at peace."*

Allow healing with each breath. With each breath, be at peace. May peace fill your body. May peace fill the depths of your being.

~

Allow your mind to think of someone to whom you feel some resentment, some lingering hurt. As they come to mind, feel the anger and the fear.

Be still in yourself. Then silently acknowledge this person and say: *"I forgive you."*

"Whatever you have done to me in the past, whatever you have done to others, whatever it was you meant to do, I forgive you."

Allow that person to rest in your mind and repeat your forgiveness.

"Whatever you have done to me in the past, whatever you have done to others, whatever it was you meant to do, I forgive you."

Then rest upon your breathing and the space within yourself.

~

Now turn in your heart again towards yourself. Return into your heart and welcome yourself silently, saying: *"I forgive you."*

Using your own name, tell your self: *"I forgive you."* No more unkindness, no more pain. Only the forgiveness that brings healing and peace.

I forgive you. May you be free from suffering. May you be at peace.

Preparing the soil

When the husband of a world famous doctor was near death, he spent an hour with her in the evenings watching films and videos of the natural world. Despite the fact that he was racked with a series of progressive illnesses, this immersion in the life of nature brought him great inner peace. After his death, his wife, too, turned to these wildlife programmes for solace. "It is really the only thing I wish to watch," she told a relative.

Closeness to nature is far more than an escape from the hustle and bustle of urban life; it is one of the most immediate ways in which we reconnect with the foundation of our being.

For countless people over the centuries, nature has been their greatest teacher and, in our struggle with life's evanescence, it is nature whose instruction in death is supreme.

Whether you are in the fullness of health or suffering from illness, the open countryside, woods, lakes and hillsides are sources of incalculable power, healing and insight. Even within the confines of a city, we can draw on that power in parks and gardens – or through images in photography and film.

The silent blossom

When a pine forest is in flames, the pine cones open and spray forth their tiny seeds onto the forest floor so that in their moment of death the future of the forest is assured in great abundance. In the same measure, our own deaths and the seemingly absurd and premature deaths of those around us seem also to hold properties like those of the kernels in the forest – of no obvious significance at the time, perhaps falling onto indifferent, smouldering ground. Yet from death itself, if we but perceive it, there can unfold, like genetic coding, a silent, subtle blossom. In its own way, as in the rest of nature, death offers us whatever we are prepared to learn.

On the shores of Walden Pond in the Massachusetts of the last century, the New England teacher and naturalist, Henry David Thoreau, built himself a cabin and lived in the woods on the expenditure of a few dollars for more than two years. His experiment and observations have earned him a unique place not only in the history of literature, but in the ranks of all those who have come to a profound understanding of death through the contemplation of nature.

"Every part of nature teaches that the passing away of one life is the making room for another," he wrote. *"The oak dies down to the ground, leaving within its rind a rich virgin mould, which will impart a vigorous life to an infant forest. So this constant abrasion and decay make the soil of our future growth."*

As he persisted with his meticulous notations, he could not help but notice the inseparability of the forms of life and death as the seasons came and went by the lakeside. Keenly attentive to the changes, he remarked on the fact that countless leaves are at their most brilliant in the period before they fall and die: *"Every fruit, on ripening, and just before its fall, acquires a bright tint. So too the leaves; so the sky before the end of the day, and the year near its setting."*

"If we see nature as pausing," he wrote, *"immediately all mortifies and decays; but seen as progressing, she is beautiful."*

ANCIENT INSTRUCTIONS
Taking and sending

The mind adjusts our pain threshold. Our thoughts and emotions radically influence the way we perceive whatever happens to us. This process affects everything we go through at the time of death.

Typically, we put up resistance to pain and avoid whatever we do not wish to accept. That resistance is often a greater source of tension, fear and trauma than the pain we are seeking to avoid. Learning to lower that resistance and to acknowledge the original pain can have remarkable effects. Like turning the light on in a dark room, we discover a power that transforms our experience of pain, both physical and mental.

The technique for re-training the mind's habitual response to pain, described on these pages, is part of the ancient Asian tradition of mental cultivation. Working with the natural rhythm of the breath, you learn a suppleness of mind which robs physical and psychological pain of its terrifying hold. You can experiment with this approach if you are faced with pain, confusion and emotional turmoil while dying, or while helping a dying person.

Breathing in

Sit or lie in a comfortable position and let your attention settle on your breathing. After a few minutes of quietude, begin to imagine that you are enveloped in dark smoke which is heavy and oppressive. As you breathe in, imagine you are deliberately taking that darkness in through every pore in your body.

Breathing out

As you breathe out, completely change the mental picture. Think of your whole body radiating lightness, ease and spaciousness.

Sustaining the cycle

Train your mind to focus on this alternating cycle of imagery for periods of several minutes. It is natural for your mind to wander or be distracted by pain while you are doing this; when you realize that you have been distracted, simply return your attention to your breathing and to the alternating sensation of darkness and light.

Your pain, others' pain

Once you have a feel for the alternating cycle, allow your feelings to rest briefly on whatever sensation, thought or emotion emerges in your mind or body as you breathe in. It can be your own pain or the pain of the person you are caring for (or who is caring for you). Simply acknowledge to yourself that you are feeling that pain or any other sensation such as anxiety. Don't analyse it or push it away. Just breathe it in.

Then breathe out, letting light and relaxation ride out on your breath as you did at the beginning. As you breathe in again, return to your inner feelings. Keep alternating with the breaths: whatever uncomfortable, dark sensation you feel as you breathe in, accept it. Then, as you exhale, let peace and spaciousness radiate outwards. Continue for five to ten minutes if possible.

Extending outwards

Whatever you experience, no matter how personal, is part of the vast drama of human life. Whatever agony you experience is a pain you share with immense numbers of other human beings, countless people who have gone before you and innumerable ones who will come after. As you breathe in, encompass everyone who is feeling and experiencing your pain. Then, as you exhale, extend to all of them feelings of lightness, clarity and spaciousness.

Letting go

This exercise may release strong feelings. This is natural. If that happens, relax. The impact of this meditation is subtle and profound. Rest quietly for a few minutes and return to it another day.

ANCIENT INSTRUCTIONS
Mingling the breaths

Breathing can be used in many ways to stabilize and direct the underlying energy of the entire body, affecting the internal organs, nervous system and mind. Although the advice given on these pages is aimed at assisting the dying person, it can be used very helpfully to support them at any time (from the time disturbing symptoms set in) and also to sustain their carers at any stage.

Working together

If the person is conscious, carefully review what you are going to do together and be sure that you are both in agreement about each stage.

The person should lie down or arrange themselves as comfortably as possible. Traditionally, the person lies on their back, with their arms resting loosely beside them. Ideally, the spine should be reasonably straight.

You should sit very near the person so that they have a good sense of your presence and can hear you when you speak. You should be sure that you can easily observe their breathing.

Ordinarily the room should be as calm and quiet as possible. But, in exceptional circumstances, it is possible to carry out this practice in a hospital ward, or at the scene of an accident. What matters is the strength of your ability to connect with the person and ignore distractions.

Relaxing the nervous system

First take time to balance your own energy, using the exercise on pages 42–3.

Then guide the person through the progressive relaxation exercise on pages 44–5. Speak calmly and clearly, taking them carefully through the structured relaxations until you have completed the full sequence.

Breathing together

Advise the person that you will now progress to the third step, mingling the breaths. Watch the person's breathing pattern very carefully. It may have an obvious rhythm. It may be erratic. Develop a sense of how to follow along with it.

Begin synchronizing your breathing with theirs. As they breathe in, you breathe in. As they breathe out, you breathe out. It is like swimming or riding, letting your relaxed body literally go with the flow.

After a few minutes, you can progress. Invite the person to say the sound "Aahhh" together with their out-breath as if sighing or expressing deep emotion. Do this together for half a dozen exhalations. Then, while they go back to breathing in silence, continue making the sound on your own, precisely timed always to coincide with the person's out-breath.

Counting

To focus attention more fully on the breathing, advise the person that you will begin counting the breaths from one to ten, over and over again, following the pattern of their breathing.

As you breathe out with them, say "One" quietly at the start of your own out-breath. Then "Two" at the start of the next and so on.

Continue with sustained precision for about 20 minutes, the period of time during which the wave patterns of the brain fully adjust to the shift in attention to the breathing.

Conclusion

Advise the person that it is time for them to become more aware of their surroundings again, to feel their head, back and legs on the bed. Ask them to touch you or to open and close their hand to signal that they are back in contact. Stay with them until their eyes are open. Take your time and remain with them for a while.

You may find it helpful to maintain physical contact with the person throughout so that they have an even stronger sense of your presence.

ANCIENT INSTRUCTIONS
Light

The spectrum of light extends across some of the most powerful energies that human beings can perceive. Light is not only energy in itself, it can also evoke or convey other energies. Throughout human civilization, it has been used as a potent force in innumerable ways and our inner resonance with light can be used to great effect when we are dying.

Light has the quality of being both energizing and soothing. It can lift our spirit, and at the same time relax us and assist the process of letting go. This is true not only of light itself, but of our internal response to mental images of light: this is the basis of the ancient art of bathing in light at the time of death. This method can also be used to supplement the relaxation and stress reduction exercises elsewhere in this book.

Enveloped in light

Resting as comfortably as possible, let your mind imagine light above your head. The energy radiates downwards so that your whole body is immersed in it.

Sense the warming quality of the light and let your mind encourage that sensation right through to your fingers and toes.

When you gradually sense that you are bathing in a pool of light, focus your attention on the top of your head. Feel that the light is entering into your body and slowly penetrating down in a straight line through the centre of your body.

If you belong to a religious or other spiritual tradition, you may choose to see the light in your mind's eye emanating from a figure of particular significance to you.

Train yourself to sustain this visualization in a relaxed, unhurried manner for several minutes at a time. If you are distracted, simply return to the idea of light and repeat the sequence.

You can extend the benefit of this practice into your life well before your death. This will make you familiar with it so that you can concentrate on it when dying. It will also give you a powerful way of relaxing your emotions in the midst of the stresses and strains of living.

Opening the doors

You can use this practice to assist a dying person throughout their illness, and particularly when they are close to death. First settle your own energy (see pages 42–3). Spend some time quietly tuning in to the person and letting your own thoughts subside. Imagine a source of light above their head and let that image of light fill your mind and envelop the person, like a warming, soft radiance. As they draw closer to death and afterwards, continue the practice, having the feeling that they are naturally and peacefully dissolving into the light.

Light for the weak

If you are too weak to be able to go through the progressive relaxation exercise on pages 44–5, which involves tensing and relaxing the various muscles groups, you may find that you can use the imagery of light instead. Whether you are doing the exercise yourself, or guiding a dying person, follow the same sequence throughout the body, but for each set of muscles, replace the instructions with these words:

"Let your [feet, back, etc.] rest very comfortably where they are and allow them to relax very fully. As you breathe out, imagine that they are bathed in soft light and that you can feel the warmth of that light. Relax as you breathe in. Then, as you breathe out, feel the light gently penetrating and warming the whole area. Relax again as you breathe in. Breathe out, sense the warm, relaxed radiance. Stay relaxed and breathe normally."

Remember that the progressive relaxation exercise is normally used before the mutual breathing practice (see page 89), so that if you are doing it with a conscious person, the light imagery will help them relax if they are very weak or tired.

ANCIENT INSTRUCTIONS

Permission to die

There is sometimes a point before death when the person finds themselves trapped in the struggle to continue living. They may be grappling with deep emotional conflicts. They may be obsessed with the need to continue living for others – to look after their children or to complete some other unfinished part of their life's work. They literally need to be given permission to die.

The following text is offered as a brief example of what you might say, and gives you a way of structuring your thoughts.

Use your own words, feeling free to reminisce about the person's life, the times you have shared together and the impact they have had on you. Remember that even a sedated person is likely to retain the power of hearing throughout the process of dying; if you are unable to speak openly to the person, and there might be many reasons for that, collect your thoughts and mentally communicate this focused energy in silence. Take your time; there is no intimacy more precious than this.

You can adapt this meditation as part of your own training for death. In some traditions it is practised daily. Through it, we begin to develop the readiness to die at any moment with our minds and hearts fully relaxed, loving and free.

Acknowledging mystery

We are both coming close to a great change. Sometimes when you are asleep I wonder if you have died. I wonder if you are at peace or in pain. I wonder what is in your heart and passing through your mind. It is not easy for me to express this, but today there is something I need you to know. It is more important than anything I have said before.

What is happening to us seems unreal and yet it is as if there is nothing more real. Everything seems so uncertain, so sad, so filled with fear. Yet there is also something very clear, very certain, very wonderful.

It is as if we were entering the mystery of your death together. Together, we are about to enter the mystery of life after you are dead.

Accepting the pain

You have been in such great pain, you have suffered more than any of us know. Your suffering brings up all the pain we have been through together and all the pain of the people around us.

There are times when the pain is so great, we feel we must have failed in some way and gone wrong somewhere in our lives. But this pain is not punishment. It is an essential part of our lives. All of it has made us what we are.

Everything we have been through together has been bringing us to this moment. Everything has been part of the design: each moment of happiness, each moment of love, each disappointment, each tragedy. It is all woven into the fabric.

Embracing peace

So much seems unfinished. So much seems ragged and incomplete. We have to let go of this pain of holding on. Whatever is left, will be taken up by others. Nothing has been lost, nothing has been wasted, nothing has been in vain. Your whole life is complete.

None of us want you to suffer for us. We don't want you to hold on for us. We don't want you to fear that you are abandoning us. We know your time has come. We want you to complete your journey. We want you to be at peace.

You are completely free. There are no chains holding you back.

The luminous universe is waiting. There is nothing more to fear.

Extending love

In the same way that none of us can possibly disappear from your life, you can never disappear from ours.

I wish I could have loved you and cared for you better. I'm doing the best I can for you now, with all my heart. I want you to die knowing that and take this love with you in your heart.

If I know that you have understood this, then the uncertainty and the sadness and the fear are all bearable. What will matter is the love we have for each other. It will be there through all the changes ahead. It is the one thing that remains clear, certain and wonderful.

Be free. Completely loved. The universe is waiting. Go in peace.

The great mantras

The focused mind is perhaps the most powerful instrument we have. At the time of death, as the energies and elements of the physical body dissipate, it may be the only instrument we have. Over the centuries various techniques have been developed to help concentrate and channel the energies of the mind so that we are able to remain anchored and at rest in the midst of the disintegration we experience in our bodies.

Most of these techniques are part of religious or mystical traditions and, as such, are often of little appeal to rationalists. But it is possible to understand the essence of these practices and put them to positive use without subscribing to the beliefs, symbols and cultural traditions associated with them.

The basic "mantra" practice is to repeat a short phrase or text with which you strongly identify – or wish to identify. It may express an ideal or a feeling. It may be part of the tradition to which you belong. It may be deeply personal and private. It may echo something in your distant past. It may be a line of poetry you love. It may be a sound that resonates within you, having no verbal content or conceptual meaning at all. Some of the world's mantras and prayers are on the facing page, but you can select or call to mind anything from your own experience that you wish to use.

The lodestar

The silent or quiet repetition of your own "mantra" becomes a potent instrument for the final concentration of your remaining mental, emotional and psychic energy. Just, as a child, you may have used a magnifying glass to focus the sun's light, you are now able to condense the mind's activity into this one-pointed simplicity.

If you wish, you can ask those close to you to share this practice with you, so that the effect of the vibration set up by the wave-like repetition fully supports you in your journey. In the mist and confusion of the last phase of living, this practice becomes your guide and its energy, your lodestar.

Mercy and Peace

Throughout the world, people assist the dying with words and prayers that invoke the spirit of peace, forgiveness and profound transformation (see facing page). *From top to bottom:* May I be free from suffering. May I be at peace
● Lord Jesus Christ, Son of God, have mercy on me
● Hear, O Israel: The Lord our God The Lord is One
● Holy Mary, Mother of God, pray for us sinners, now, and in the hour of our death ● May Infinite Compassion transform the suffering of all beings
● Whatever may come to pass is the Will of Allah, the Merciful and Compassionate.
Left side: May the Great Buddha of Compassion be my guide, the embodiment of enlightened, limitless love.
Bottom: for centuries the symbol OM has been chanted as an invocation of the supreme spiritual power of the universe perpetually manifest in each of us without beginning or end.

南嘸阿彌陀佛

MAY I BE FREE FROM SUFFERING.
MAY I BE AT PEACE.

Господи Иисусе Христе, Сыне Божий, помилуй мя грешного.

שְׁמַע יִשְׂרָאֵל יְיָ אֱלֹהֵינוּ יְיָ אֶחָד׃

Sancta Maria, Mater Dei, ora pro nobis peccatoribus, nunc et in hora mortis nostrae. Amen.

ཨོཾ་མ་ཎི་པདྨེ་ཧཱུྃ༔

إِنْ شَاءَ اللّٰه

ॐ

At the time of death

It should be a sacred day for you when one of your people dies – a sacred day when a soul is released and returns to its home.

BLACK ELK

The dying person should be enveloped in an atmosphere of serenity, respect and love. This is the advice of virtually all spiritual traditions. It may prove impossible if the death is abrupt, accidental or violent, in which case other practices may be needed after the death.

If it is possible to be with the person at the time of death, they should be encouraged to remain in a relaxed, tranquil state of mind. The practice of 'mingling the breaths', explained on pages 148–9, can be a very powerful support for this. In some esoteric traditions it is used as a way of taking the person through the death transition, providing close companionship at that stage of the journey and calming any emotional and physical turbulence. If several people are involved in the caring, it is best for one person to be principally responsible for ensuring continuity of the practice.

Mingling your breathing is a profound form of human sharing. It is intimate, uncluttered and mutually strengthening. It automatically directs attention away from distractions and towards the fundamental experience you are both going through.

Doctors and counsellors who work with the dying underline the value of this practice. "In the last stages of dying," observes one counsellor, "the lungs often fill up and the person dies of congestive heart failure. This breathing practice induces a deep state of relaxation, slowing oxygen requirements. It is a way to die in peace, joy, harmony and dignity, without drugs or euthanasia. It is the most loving gift you can give to anyone."

The last touch

In some traditions you are advised to allow the body of a dead person to remain untouched for at least three days, since the complete process of dying extends beyond clinical certification of death. If the person has requested that such a period of complete stillness be observed, you should make advance arrangements so that their wish is respected.

If that is not practicable, the advice is that the first and, initially, only area of the body to be touched after death should be the very top of the head, gently, calmly and in the spirit of wishing the person well on their journey. In the esoteric traditions, it is through the tiny aperture at the top of the head, variously known as the fontanelle, meeting point or thousand-petalled lotus, that the consciousness is liberated at the time of death, ideally under the guidance of a spiritual master. Since this may occur spontaneously, the advice to followers of such systems is not to disturb the inner flow of energy by touching the person at any other point of the body immediately after death.

In some cultures, it is an essential part of the religious ritual for the relatives to sit with and then wash and prepare the body after death. In some hospices, relatives are involved in washing and dressing the dead person so that they can fully engage in a final, cathartic farewell to the body.

Honouring the body

One carer has described her experience of being with the dead person in these words:

"I was alone in the room with the body for three hours after his death and was able to massage his body with the oil with which I had massaged him when he was well. I was able to hold him, to stroke him, to remember what we had gone through together. I went through the whole gamut of emotions in those hours and it made me realize just what we are deprived of when we hand the body over to a mortician or funeral director without honouring the relationship which has just passed in the form that we recognize it. It is in this body that the relationships that we have on this level take place and it's important to honour the body that contains the spirit which we recognize in each other."

PART FIVE

The return journey

FAREWELLS

·

REMEMBRANCES

·

THE UNEXPECTED

Nothing in the entire universe ever perishes, believe me, but things vary and assume new forms. Though one thing changes into another and that also changes, yet the sum of everything remains unchanged.

PYTHAGORAS

Those we love

Thousands of people in countries all over the world have "disappeared". They have been abducted by the secret police, held in secret detention and murdered because of their beliefs. Rarely have their lovers and relatives been able to trace them, to bury their bodies or to grieve fully for them. Many of the bereaved families have managed to make new lives for themselves; others have not. In the words of one: "I refuse to let my sister be forgotten and to carry on as if nothing had happened. That would be to give her murderers the final victory."

For countless other people who have experienced the death of someone they love, those words may speak to something very deep inside them, even if the circumstances of the deaths were very different. For them, their grief may be a determined and necessary act of remembrance to ensure that the dead person's life remains cherished and to prevent death robbing that life of the value it had. For some, their grief may be the expression of an inconsolable loss: the person who died meant so much to them that their own life has been irreparably diminished.

The healing model

We are often anxious to do something for people in deep grief, to ease their pain, to show how much we care. However, just as with the dying, it is important not to impose our assumptions on the bereaved. We may have trouble witnessing their grief because of the unresolved pain it reflects in our own lives. At times we risk trivializing the importance of their grief by encouraging them "to get over it" or using polite euphemisms about the death. Although we often speak of the need to heal the wounds of grief, we may fail to understand that some deaths change a person forever.

❀

Aromatherapy for paralysing grief

•

Use one or more of:
bergamot
frankincense
lavender
sweet marjoram
melissa
or ylang ylang
in a bath, as an inhalation
or in a vaporizer.

•

Instructions for use are on pages 26–7.

❀

Let tears flow of their own accord: their flowing is not inconsistent with inward peace and harmony.

SENECA

A sense of integration

Seventeen years after the death of her small son, Simon, Dee Cooper wrote movingly of her feelings. Her words are a powerful reminder that grief is intensely personal, does not conform to theoretical models and can be fully integrated into human life without either fear or shame.

"After many years of bewilderment I have come to the conclusion that the feelings that result from the death of a child are not resolvable. They continue, are painful, are re-experienced at intervals, and this is the normal pattern. I also see no place for the word reintegration. The death of a child changes your life irrevocably. There is no going back. The prefix 're-' is wrong. What I have experienced is a sense of integration. My feelings about Simon are part of my life. The initially fearful recognition that literally anything could happen to me or those I love at any moment has been enriching. I live more in the present. I experience each moment at a deeper level than I would previously have thought possible. Experiencing and feeling are enhanced. I am both sadder and happier than I was before.

I suspect that models and frameworks of grief and words like resolution and reintegration have more to do with professionals containing their anxieties than reality. I intend to be honest about my sad days in future. If you have the courage to be confronted by reality – the reality that the world is not a safe place, the reality that children can die, the reality that the pain of grief can be lasting – then do ask me how I am.
I think that the quality of my life has been enhanced by this knowledge; perhaps yours could be."

Living with grief

Loss, grief and stress sap our energy. After the shock of death, and the anger and other emotions that are released, there can be a deep sense of depression, apathy and exhaustion. Life seems tedious, pointless and sometimes intensely irritating.

The risk is that you begin to consume your own life, draining yourself emotionally and physically, and to allow the poisons of bitterness and self-hatred to insinuate their way into everything you do. This is not grieving: it is not honouring the life of the person who has died, nor making your remaining days a fitting tribute to them.

Self-destructive tendencies can and do emerge in the process of grief. Thankfully, as it becomes permissable to re-admit death to our society, there are self-help methods, voluntary groups and professionals who can help people deal constructively with such forces (see Resources, pages 184–7). You may also find that the mental and physical exercises in the earlier parts of this book are helpful to keep your internal balance while adjusting to living with grief.

Not everyone

There is no universal model for grief. We react to loss in very different ways. What for some people is a devastating event, may for others be natural and unremarkable. The emotions evoked by the death even of a lifelong partner are rooted in the depths of our personality and our most fundamental attitudes to life. We may feel no inclination to grieve at all if we see their death as a natural, fitting and positive conclusion to a life well spent. We may have spiritual beliefs which transcend normal perceptions of loss and grief. In some cases, the person's death may be a final relief from years of suffering. On the other hand, people's hearts can be broken, irretrievably and in silence. We know so little from the outside, we should be wary of our assumptions about each other's grief.

Star of Bethlehem
This is the flower essence recommended for easing the effects of grief and sorrow. It can also be helpful if the person has difficulty expressing their grief.
It is a powerful support in times of shock and is included in the Rescue Remedy (see page 165).

Bereavement is the deepest initiation into
the mysteries of human life.

DEAN INGE

The dead in the midst of the living

If you were to die in Mexico, you would know that you would
be "called back" each year on the Day of the Dead. Ancient
Aztec rituals fuse with local Roman Catholic customs to create a
celebration far removed from the denial of death so prevalent
elsewhere. Throughout the country on 2 November, families
"welcome back" their dead with offerings of food, drink and
music. The favourite foods of the deceased are set out for them
and their photos displayed on special altars in people's homes.
Calaveras, "living" skeletons, thread their way through the
streets, mingling with the population. They play merry
instruments, and take part in weddings and dances. A particular
emphasis is placed on including children in the festival, linking
death with their toys and candies – reflecting the traditional
Amerindian custom of exposing children to the facts and
rituals of death.

Unexpected deaths

The approach of death automatically triggers our conditioned responses to extreme danger. Even to a person who has been ill, the prognosis of a terminal condition is like a mortal blow.

This is all the more true when we are confronted by news that someone we know has dropped dead, been killed in an accident or violent attack, or committed suicide. In such situations, we may find ourselves waiting in the emergency ward of a hospital, visiting a morgue, dealing with the police and the news media. At the same time we must cope not only with our own powerful emotions, but those of other distraught and angry people as well. People in such situations most commonly tend to exhibit symptoms of withdrawal, denial, anger and isolation. This further complicates communications with medical and other professionals, and with others who are undergoing the same trauma. In that maelstrom, familiarity with death practices can be of immense value.

For the person who has died

The practices recommended throughout this book to assist a dying person also apply to a person who is dying abruptly and without warning, or is already dead. Should you happen to be called to the bedside of someone who is very near death, in a coma, unconscious or on life support equipment, remember that normally the senses of feeling and hearing are the last to go. You can touch them and speak to them, since it is highly likely that what you are doing is being felt and heard even if there is no obvious response. You can apply any of the Ancient Instructions (pages 146–53).

If the person is already dead, there may be certain cultural or religious requirements that should be respected. You may also wish to acknowledge the death in your own way, bearing in mind that there is a considerable body of traditional wisdom which holds that consciousness is not annihilated by the death of the body. The practices of 'taking and sending' (pages 146–7), 'light' (pages 150–1), 'permission to die' (pages 152–3), and the advice on what to do at the time of death (pages 156–7) are all applicable, and can also transform the emotional energy experienced by all who are present.

❁

*Aromatherapy
for crisis*

•

In the event of a sudden crisis, your nervous system may respond positively to inhaling 4 drops of lavender or neroli oil on a tissue. You can also add the following blend to a warm bath to help relieve tension and encourage a good night's sleep:

•

2 drops of geranium
2 drops of lavender
2 drops of sandalwood
1 drop of ylang ylang

❁

Nature's response to shock and trauma

Our bodies and minds have a remarkable ability to respond to startling and extreme events. However, at such times we often find ourselves in environments and social settings where our innate ability to restore equilibrium is seriously impaired. There are natural remedies that you may find extremely helpful: if you are trying to cope with the intense distress caused by the sudden or violent death of someone you love; if you have yourself been a survivor of an incident in which others have died; or if you are trying to support someone in these circumstances.

The Bach Rescue Remedy

Some practitioners and followers of complementary therapies carry a small bottle of this with them at all times. It is a combination of Cherry Plum, Clematis, Impatiens, Rock Rose and Star of Bethlehem; it is an all-purpose emergency composite for the effects of anguish. It is used for those who have been seriously distressed and risk falling into a numbed state of mind. It has a calming, comforting and reassuring effect on the nervous system, allowing the natural healing energies within the person to work without hindrance.

Place four drops of the liquid in a cup of water, which should be sipped at intervals.

Inner work

'Mingling the breaths' (see pages 148–9) and 'taking and sending' (see pages 146–7) can be immensely valuable in these situations. However, the full benefit can only be obtained if you have become thoroughly familiar with these practices already – underlining the fact that the unfolding of wisdom includes one's personal preparation for the unexpected, both in order to help oneself and to be of immediate assistance to others.

IN THE MIRROR

Are you living on the assumption that no accidents will happen to you, that you are unlikely to be the victim of violence or that you are immune from fatal illness?

Have you had a frank discussion with your family or your loved ones about what would need to be done if any of you were to die or be killed?

Have you prepared a Will (see pages 134–5), a Living Will (see pages 136–7) and a Death File (see page 130)?

Young deaths

The death of a child tests us to the limits of our being. Many parents feel they die themselves if their child dies, or they liken it to an amputation, even to the complete loss of their own desire to live. With the death of a child, it can feel as if the future has died, too.

A child's death also evokes profound feelings of personal responsibility, failure and guilt. Bereft parents often blame themselves for not meeting their "sacred obligation" to raise and protect their children. They find themselves drowned in an overwhelming sense of worthlessness.

Precisely because the death of a child seems to violate the natural order, those most affected feel compelled to find an acceptable explanation for it. They may scan their own lives and all events associated with the child's death obsessively, looking for clues as if they were solving a murder. Underlying that search can be a deep-seated desire to apportion blame. All too often that ends up with the parents mercilessly accusing themselves. This is true whether it be a stillbirth, a cot death, a death in infancy or childhood, or a death that at any stage in life precedes the death of the parents.

Family members may withdraw into their individual grief. They simply cannot bear to discuss the death or their deep feelings with one another, and find themselves unable to break the silence or deal with each other's pain. A double burden is borne by the grandparents who must face their own grief at the loss of the child, and witness, often helplessly, the agony of the parents.

The pressure on the parents may be increased by other people's expectations that they will "get over it in time". Experience shows that the death of your child is something you always carry with you.

Surviving children in the family and the friends of the dead child may be very deeply affected. Those parents are then presented with the challenge of discussing death with their children and acting as counsellors.

The flame is like a human,
It lives and dies.
Its life is a wild impetuous one
During its span — it frolics dances and
Appears to have a carefree existence.
Although it might be joyous in a short period
It has a tragic death
The tragedy is in its struggle not to die.

A 12-YEAR-OLD BOY, ONE
YEAR BEFORE HIS DEATH

Where to turn

Not everyone has these reactions. Your views, feelings and circumstances may be very different. Whatever your experience, you may find the advice and therapies in this book helpful, whether for yourself, for a dying young person or in supporting their carers. There is also a growing number of organizations and professionals now working to help those dealing with the death of a young person, such as Compassionate Friends. You can contact these groups using the Resources (pages 184–7).

As a friend

If you want to give support to someone grieving the death of a child, come to them bearing no hidden agenda of healing, no time scale for their return to normality, no solution for their pain.

If ever there was a time to put aside your insistence on your own beliefs and your own ideas about how people should grieve, this is it. Come open handed. Be present, listen intently and they will take your hand if they wish.

IN THE MIRROR

Despite the fact that there are now several groups providing support and advice to those affected by the death of a child, there are still questions we can all ask ourselves, whether parents or not, about our own attitudes:

What assumptions do you make about the extent to which you can protect children from death?

What answers would you give to a child who asks you about death and about what will happen when you die and they die?

It should not be considered morbid to dwell on these questions. They can arise at any time, either directly or as a result of disasters or other tragedies reported in the news media. It is one of the greatest acts of love and compassion to examine these realities with an open heart.

The three questions

Little Arya's mother was seriously ill in hospital. On the only occasion when the child had visited her there, he had been so terrified by all the equipment around the bedside he had never been able to go back. Now she was near death and the parents asked a counsellor to assist them by talking to the little boy.

The counsellor asked Arya three questions.

"Do you realize your mother is dying?"

"What does that mean?" replied Arya.

"It means she will not be coming home. She will not be able to look after you any more. She will not be able to do any of the things with you that she used to. You will never see her again."

The little boy was silent. The counsellor was silent too for some time. Then he asked his second question:

"What does that feel like to you?"

"Very sad," said Arya. "Very lonely."

The counsellor was silent for a long time. Then he asked his third question:

"What do you want to do about that?"

After a while, the boy described to the counsellor exactly how he would like to say goodbye to his mother, what he wanted to do at her funeral and how he would like to remember her in the years ahead.

As a result of those three questions and the ensuing unconditional silences, the little boy's responses emerged with precision and honesty. His innate ability to be direct and creative had been unlocked.

You may already be asking yourself the fourth question: "Shouldn't we try to do that for everyone and not only for our children?"

Whenever there is a death in the family, the three questions are a way forward. They go straight to the heart of the matter, enabling us to acknowledge the reality of death in terms of our own experience, giving us permission to feel the emotional impact of the event and allowing us to express ourselves in a meaningful way.

Do not stand at my grave and weep;
I am not there. I do not sleep.

I am a thousand winds that blow.
I am the diamond glints on snow.
I am the sunlight on ripened grain.
I am the gentle autumn's rain.

When you awaken in the morning's hush,
I am the swift uplifting rush
Of quiet birds in circled flight.
I am the soft stars that shine at night.

Do not stand at my grave and cry;
I am not there, I did not die.

ANON

Broken journeys

We often say that life is a journey. Some see
it as a pilgrimage.

What happens if we get lost on our
way? What happens if we are overtaken by
terrifying events, enveloped in perpetual
despair or caught in the grip of ceaseless
pain? We may give up all hope of ever
reaching the holy site to which we have
made our life's pilgrimage.

Whether you see life's journey as a
one-off voyage from birth to death, or
as part of a greater existence that
continues beyond death, you may be
faced at any time with issues surrounding a
suicide or assisted suicide.

"Personal holocaust"

The reasons that lead a person to commit suicide are
as numerous and complex as the thousands of people
who do so each year. You may regard suicide as a
morally indefensible act, a personal tragedy or a
powerful personal decision, but few events in life
have the same impact on us as the suicide of a friend
or loved one.

Those who have been close to someone who
committed suicide now describe themselves as
"survivors"; one said the experience was her
"personal holocaust". The feelings of grief can be
overwhelming, particularly the sense of guilt and
anger. Such survivors frequently insist that they are
somehow to blame, obsessively asking themselves:
"Why didn't she contact me before taking her own
life? Why didn't I realize she was in such pain?"

These questions remain forever unanswered and
the survivors rarely find anyone willing to talk to
them about the event or their continuing plight.
They may suffer in silence for years. When they find
someone they can talk to, or if finally they feel the
time has come to end their silence – and if you are
the person to whom they speak – for them what
matters most is the quality of your listening and your
willingness to understand, without argument or
judgment, the pain from which they have yet to
be released.

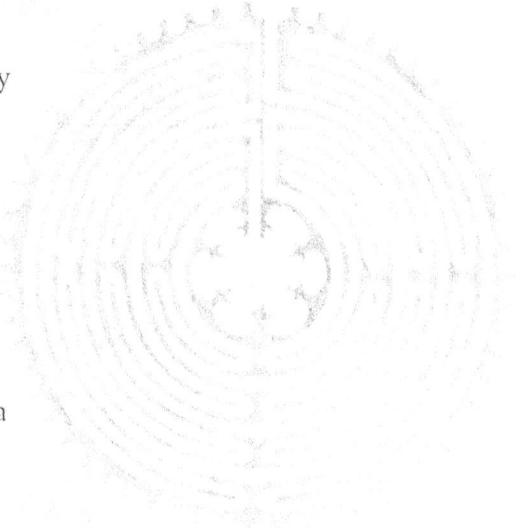

The great labyrinth on the
floor of Chartres Cathedral is
a poignant expression of our
life's journey. Pilgrims who
could not go to Jerusalem
followed its twists and turns
on their knees. Trace its path
with your finger. Each turn,
whether confusing or difficult, whether away from or
towards the centre, is always
taking us to the same point.
Every experience is part of
the journey: the centre of
the labyrinth is always
waiting for us, regardless of
our confusion, pain or
uncertainty.

Prolonging life artificially

Some people who find themselves trapped in an experience of intense pain may decide to end their lives and ask doctors or others to help them die. "Mercy killings" grab headlines and become the subject of sensational court cases. But in fact a growing trend in contemporary medical practice requires doctors and relatives to take similar decisions. This is largely the consequence of technology that can prolong life artificially, and raises the question of how long to continue such life support (for example, in persistent vegetative state, or PVS).

In trying to navigate through the ethical questions involved, two ways of seeing the issue have become common in hospitals. One is to make a distinction between actions and omissions: no action will be taken to terminate the person's life, but they will not be given further treatment to prolong it unnaturally. Another approach is to weigh up the burdens and benefits to the person of further active treatment. Both, however, require someone to make the final decision, usually when the person in question is incapable of participating. It can be harrowing for the relatives to try to decide what is in the best interests of their loved one and this is when an Advance Directive or Living Will (see pages 136–7) becomes so valuable as a clear statement of what the person wishes to have happen under such circumstances.

Intense pain, confusion and sorrow occur at deep levels of our being. It is not always possible to make contact with the person through language and argument. But there is almost always a part of the total consciousness of the person that is open to and aware of human contact – through touch, empathetic breathing and the other practices that are offered throughout this book.

The changed person

While a person's journey through life may be terminated by their own decision or with the assistance of others, a particularly harrowing phenomenon is the continuation of bodily life but the apparently involuntary transformation of the personality. This is associated in its most acute form with Alzheimer's disease. The person's behaviour becomes inconsistent and unmanageable, and they may finally cease to recognize or relate in any normal way to their relatives and carers. Without that spark of recognition it becomes almost impossible for carers to continue to bear the burden and the person is usually given into professional care.

Saying goodbye

Sing your death song and die like a hero going home.

SHAWNEE PEOPLE SAYING

Some people regard a corpse as a used body and see no reason for a funeral or memorial service of any sort. Others expect their body to be interred or cremated in accordance with their religion.

Many other people are unsure what to do, avoid the question entirely and leave their relatives or loved ones to make all such decisions.

A rite of passage

Whatever your views on how to dispose of a dead body, the fact remains that the transformation of a living person into a lifeless one is not insignificant. Most cultures have developed rituals of some form to mark the event – and all serve a range of purposes.

Funerals and memorials are one way in which we seek to pay our respects to the person who has died. Even if you are someone who has no wish to have a service of any sort after your death, those who have loved you and known you may still feel the need to acknowledge your death and say goodbye in their own way. The absence of a formal ceremony to mourn a person's death does not in any way diminish the value of their life, but it is worth reflecting on the potential aspects of such events:

The fact of the death is openly acknowledged.

The nature and trauma of the death can be placed in the context of the person's entire life.

The values, human qualities and achievements of the dead person can be recalled and celebrated.

The loss and grief of the survivors can be legitimately and publicly expressed.

Those who need the support of others can draw strength from the presence and well wishes of friends, family and the community.

The power of the event itself may stir reflections that have a long-lasting impact on all involved.

Your farewell checklist

What do you want done with your body – burial, cremation or donation to medical science? (see pages 134–5)

What do you feel would be the most appropriate way for people to say goodbye to you after your death?

Do you want people to be able to say goodbye in ways other than a funeral or memorial service? How?

If you are a great lover of nature, would you like your friends and family to gather outdoors, at one of your favourite locations?

Is there anything you want said or read at your funeral?

Would you prefer silence?

Are there people you would like to be present?

Do you want someone in particular to lead the gathering?

Is it to be a party or some other form of celebration?

Are there particular values or human qualities you want emphasized?

Is there an important cause or charity you want to benefit?

If you want to be cremated, where would you like your ashes to be scattered?

Thinking ahead

Having a funeral or collective memorial service is by no means the only way in which to say goodbye to a dead person or to give support to those who need it. But a decision on whether to have a funeral service and, if so, what kind of service, does need to be made. And if it is to be *your funeral* and you want to be involved in the decision-making, then you have to think about it and preferably discuss it with those who will be involved *while you are still able to do so.* Avoiding the issue almost inevitably means the decision will be left until after your death, taken in a fraught atmosphere and can even result in painful conflict between family members and friends.

A rare opportunity

Thinking about the disposal of your body and saying goodbye can help focus the mind on the most important values of your life and your relations with other people. It can be an extremely powerful and affirmative subject to discuss with someone you are close to (whether you are talking about your own death or theirs).

Those who work with the dying have found that it can be very therapeutic and ennobling for the person to plan the details of whatever sort of event they would find meaningful (see checklist opposite). Great creativity and honesty is often expressed. At the moment of writing, one terminally ill woman has made plans for a party at which her friends will paint brilliantly coloured designs on her coffin before she is buried. Others have found they could express great dignity by asking for their funeral to be conducted as simply as possible, a natural moment in the perpetual cycle of birth and death.

Green burials

Many of our conventional methods for dealing with dead bodies have been challenged by the environmental movement. Burial in cemeteries puts pressure on land use and wastes coffin woods and metals. Cremation wastes wood and energy, and releases acids and other pollutants into the atmosphere. However, because of the grip of the funeral industry, most people are at a loss to know what alternatives are available.

Thanks to the natural death movement, green burials are now possible. A person can be buried in a bio-degradable coffin, fabric or a willow woven chrysalis in an area designated to become woodland. Rather than a headstone, a tree is planted so that the land will eventually become forest, forming an undisturbed habitat for plants and wildlife. Farmers, local authorities and nature charities are beginning to establish Woodland or Nature Reserve Burial Grounds. The Natural Death Centre (see Resources, pages 184–7) in the UK is aiming to establish an Association of Nature Reserve Burial Grounds.

Garden burials

To be legal, all burials involve some formalities, including registering the death. But often what we think (and are told) is legally required, is not. In the UK, despite widespread misinformation from official bodies, you can bury your loved ones in your garden without a coffin and without the services of an undertaker. All you require under the law is a Certificate of Disposal from the Registrar of Births and Deaths or an Order for Burial from the Coroner.

Garden burials have been given the go-ahead by some local councils, and an exhaustive study of UK legislation carried out by the Natural Death Centre has established that there is nothing in British law that either forbids garden burials or requires people to obtain permission for them. This has been confirmed by the Department of the Environment who simply advise that you append a plan of where the body is to the deeds for your property. You may also consult the National Rivers Authority to ensure that you are not polluting the water table.

We are laid asleep
In body, and become a living soul:
While with an eye made quiet by the power
Of harmony, and the deep power of joy,
We see into the life of things.

WILLIAM WORDSWORTH

Remembrance

The dead are of great importance to us. They have shaped and shared our lives. We carry their imprint in our psyches, whether they be our ancestors, our immediate family or those we have known, worked with, and loved. In the words of an old Chinese saying, "We are the same blood".

The natural heritage of human culture includes the remembrance of the dead. Virtually all societies have evolved formal and informal rituals for it. Most of us partake in these in some way, at some time, consciously or unconsciously. But many people, particularly in highly industrialized societies, find that traditional forms of remembrance do not correspond to their needs or world view. That is no reason, however, to disregard the importance of finding meaningful ways of sustaining our inherent connection with those who have died.

More and more people are now experimenting with their own forms of remembrance and releasing creativity and healing energy in the process.

Your own healing

Reflecting on the fullness of an entire lifetime helps to lift a dying person out of the claustrophobia of their immediate illness and death. If you are facing your own death, you are likely to find it extremely constructive and liberating, both for yourself and for your family and friends, to talk about about how you would like to be remembered. This serves as a precious opportunity to remind everyone of the values that are of greatest importance to you and how you would wish the memory of you to nourish those values in their lives.

Remember, however, that we are all putting our memorials in place day by day. It is the way we live our lives and the way we care for others that ultimately determines the memories we leave behind and the human qualities for which we are remembered. In the words of Dag Hammarskjöld: "Do not seek death. Death will find you. But seek the road which makes death a fulfilment."

*Death
not merely
ends life,
it also bestows
upon it
a silent
completeness,
snatched from
the hazardous flux
to which all
human beings
are subject.*

HANNAH ARENDT

Ideas for the future

Fresh innovations are being made all the time as people find new ways to express respect and affection for their dead loved ones.

At home you can:
• set aside some space as a small "gallery" with a changing display of items the person collected and their favourite pieces of art and photography, for visitors and friends to share.

• observe the relevant religious or cultural rituals which mark significant phases of time after the person's death. Thereafter declare an annual memorial holiday in their honour to be celebrated by friends and relatives with outings, feasts and fireworks.

In honour of the person, you can:
• create your own work of art, commission a work of art or develop a collective work done by all who knew them.

• plant trees, make a contribution to a nature reserve or arrange to care for or feed animals for which the person had a particular affection.

• make a significant donation to a charity that reflects the person's ideals and values or launch a public campaign in their memory to improve some aspect of public life about which they were concerned.

Together with others, you can:
• create a Memory Box which could contain contributions from people who knew the dead person, such as items that have special significance, written tributes, letters and drawings.

• make a video which serves as a biography of, or tribute to, the person; one award-winning suggestion is to incorporate such a video facility into the "tombstone of tomorrow".

Our global memory
An Internet "Garden of Remembrance" has been opened on an Internet World Wide Web site: DeathNET. You can place a memorial on the site and it will be displayed according to your wishes. What you are doing is depositing a creative imprint of the dead person in the global memory of the future. You can design any message you wish, with photos of the person, sequences from home videos and tributes from friends. You can update it or change it as often as you wish. The internet address is: <http://www.islandnet.com/deathnet/garden.html>

Exuberant deaths

For some individuals, facing death and going through the death process can be a time of heightened consciousness, of joy, enthusiasm and liberation. Sometimes we see this attitude in the plans people make for their funerals – often leaving money in their wills for a magnificent party to which they want all their friends invited. And funeral rituals in various societies are by no means entirely sad and solemn. Irish wakes are famous the world over, as are the blaring jazz bands that accompany funeral processions in New Orleans.

The spirit of exuberant death is a wholehearted embrace of the totality of existence, far removed from the fearful view of death that has become so prevalent. If that spirit is to illuminate our experience of dying and our reaction to the deaths of others, it cannot be conjured up simply at the point of encountering death. It blossoms forth spontaneously, born from the way we have chosen to live our entire lives.

The death song of St Francis

St Francis of Assisi, the 13th-century Italian saint, lived an exemplary life of poverty and service, and at its end was taken to the palace of his Bishop. According to one of his biographers, his final days were remarkable:

St Francis, wanting to know how long he had to live, asked the doctor, who avoided a direct answer for some time but finally said that the disease was incurable and that he might die soon. St Francis, overjoyed, raised his hands and cried, "Welcome, Sister Death!". He bade farewell to his friends and friars and dictated some letters. A few days later, near to death, he asked the doctor to announce the arrival of Sister Death. "She will open for me the door of life," he explained. Then, following his instructions, the Franciscan brothers spread a coarse cloth on the ground, placed their mentor on it and sprinkled him with dust and ashes. St Francis was heard to mutter faintly the 142nd Psalm. After that he struggled to sing his own Canticle of the Creatures:

> And Death is our sister, we praise thee for Death
> Who releases the soul to the light of Thy gaze;
> And dying we cry with the last of our breath
> Our thanks and our praise.

His voice failed at that moment. He died singing the praise of death.

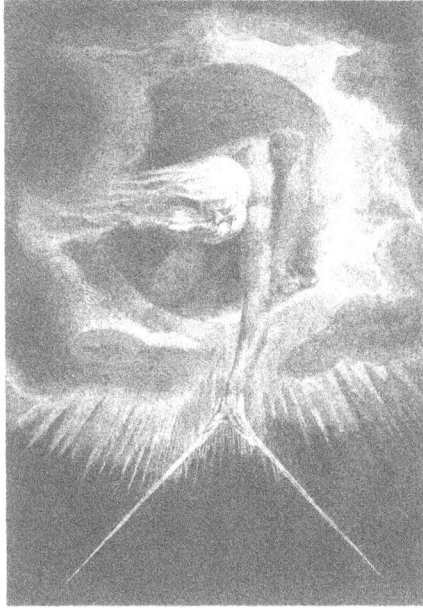

The last moments of William Blake

The extraordinary insight and vision of William Blake, the 18th-century English poet and engraver, transformed his life's work into an enduring fount of inspiration.

He was born into a family of London stocking makers and had no formal education. By the time of his death, at age 70, he had created a vast body of mystical poetry and symbolic art, embracing not only the order of the Universe, but also the tumultuous events of his day which saw democratic revolutions in both France and America. Throughout his life Blake, artist and champion of freedom, perceived an all-pervading presence of divine sympathy and love shining through even the darkest moments of suffering and sorrow: "the real and eternal world of which the Vegetable Universe is but a faint shadow".

On the day of his death, he called his wife to his bedside and said: "Kate, you have been a good wife. I will draw your portrait." According to the records of the time, she sat by the bed and her husband sketched. He began to sing "hallelujahs & songs of joy & Triumph. He sang loudly and with true ecstatic energy and seemed, too, happy that he had finished his course, that he had run his race & that he was shortly to arrive at the Goal."

"Just before he died his countenance became fair. His eyes Brighten'd and he burst out into Singing of the things he saw in Heaven."

Back from the dead

An extraordinary number of people around the world have returned from apparent clinical death to describe what are now known as "near-death experiences". The evidence is so overwhelming, crossing all cultural, racial, religious and other distinctions, that it has become the subject of extensive international scientific investigation. Although the vast majority of people report intensely uplifting experiences like those described on the facing page, not everyone does. Some people talk of feelings of panic, loneliness and gloom. But all speak of reaching a turning point at which they either chose or were instructed to return to life.

The experience is so powerful that most people say that it transformed their lives, giving them a sense of freedom, greatly reducing their fear of death and making them far more open and compassionate towards others.

The scientific rationale

While it is a fact that near-death experiences occur, there is dispute about what causes them. Some people interpret them as proof of life after death.

Other investigators see them as the result of the brain being starved of oxygen. The peaceful feeling indicates decreased nerve activity; chemical changes in the brain result in the sense of body separation; when these affect the visual cortex, the experience of darkness begins; visual hallucinations result in seeing the light; and when the part of the brain responsible for consciousness is directly affected we feel we are entering the light.

Psychological interpretations explain the experience as the way in which our ego projects its fantasies on the process of dying. Like the biological interpretation, this is based on the view that the death of the brain is the death of all consciousness.

Whichever interpretation you find appropriate, the majority of those people who have reported near-death experiences are consistent in describing a sequence of events which is overwhelming in its magnetic intensity. In the words of one scientific investigator, they have returned from the portals of death anointed by "an ineffable truth encountered face to face at death's closest moments".

What happens after death is so unspeakably glorious that our imagination and feelings do not suffice to form even an approximate conception of it.

CARL JUNG

In their own words

"There is no feeling you experience in normal life that is anything like this."

~

*"Hovering beneath the ceiling, I looked down
Upon a body; untenanted – my own
Strangely at peace, airy, weightless as light,
I floated there freed from pain-filled days and nights."*

~

"I was in what felt like outer space. It was absolutely black out there and I felt like I was being drawn towards an opening like at the end of a tunnel. I know this because I could see a light at the end; that's how I knew it was there. I know it wasn't a dream, dreams don't happen that way. I never once imagined it was a dream."

~

"I went forward towards the light and as I did so I had such a feeling of freedom and joy, it's beyond words to explain. I had a boundless sense of expansion."

~

"This light was so total and complete that you didn't look at the light, you were the light."

~

" When I came out of the coma in the hospital, I opened my eyes and saw pieces of the Light everywhere. I could see how everything in the world fits together."

~

"I used to worry about life and living and trying to get ahead. I don't do that anymore. I've been through death and it didn't bother me. I'm not scared of it."

A world culture

The wellsprings of the alternative way of death lie in some of humanity's oldest civilizations. There has been a profound conviction at the heart of the European tradition, from Socrates to the present day, that the contemplation of death, far from being morbid, has immense power to transform our lives.

In a letter to his father, Wolfgang Amadeus Mozart spoke for that tradition when he wrote: "As death, strictly speaking, is the true goal of our lives, I have for some years past been making myself so familiar with this truest and best friend that its aspect has not only ceased to appal me, but I find it very soothing and comforting! And I thank my God that He has vouchsafed me the happiness of an opportunity (you will understand) to recognize it as the key to our true bliss. I never lie down to sleep without reflecting that (young as I am) I may perhaps not see another day – yet none of those who know me can say that I am morose or melancholy in society – and I thank my Creator every day for this happiness and wish from the bottom of my heart that all others might share it."

The god Shiva, one of the three principal deities of Hinduism; his dance of destruction is an act of creation.

The ancient treasure house

To the ancients as well, death was part of a vast cycle of continuous creation. In the rock paintings of the first peoples of Australasia we find a cosmology in which the individual's death is one event in a far longer journey of being. We find this same vision in Minoan mythology, the rituals of Inuit shamans and the beliefs of the European Celts.

Traditional Chinese medicine, Indian Ayurvedic medicine and Tibetan health practices all incorporate a philosophy that places death within the vast cycle of cosmic existence. The link between living and dying is expressed in the Hindu tradition by the great god Shiva, the Lord of Destruction, who is also the Lord of Creation. Without the full trauma and pain of annihilation, the perpetual recreation of the Universe would not be possible.

"I try to follow in his footsteps"

The alternative tradition is not the private preserve of philosophers, musicians and shamans. It is the birthright of all individuals. In this extract from an account of the last months of Helen Nearing's husband, she describes how his affectionate and composed death became an inspiration.

"A month or two before he died he was sitting at table with us at a meal. Watching us eat he said, 'I think I won't eat any more.' 'All right,' I said. 'I understand. I think I would do that too. Animals know when to stop. They go off in a corner and leave off food.'

So I put Scott on juices ... He got weaker, of course, and was as gaunt and thin as Gandhi ... He was bed-ridden and had little strength but spoke with me daily ...when it seemed he was slipping away, I sat beside him on his bed.

We were quiet together; no interruptions, no doctors or hospitals. I said, 'It's all right, Scott. Go right along. You've lived a good life and are finished with things here. Go on and up – up into the light. We love you and let you go. It's all right.'

In a soft voice, with no quiver of pain or disturbance he said, 'all right ...all right', and breathed slower and slower and slower till there was no movement any more and he was gone out of his body as easily as a leaf drops from the tree in autumn, slowly twisting and falling to the ground...

As to myself and my old age: I try to follow in his footsteps. It is not easy homesteading alone, but I carry on. A few more years and I also will experience the great Transition. May I live halfway as good a life and die as good a death."

RESOURCES

Death is much more openly discussed than ever. A useful range of books, tapes and videos is becoming available on various aspects of dying and bereavement. Organizations, professional counsellors and small self-help groups are now active in many countries to provide support and advice to people facing death.

Understanding death

Bowker, John *The Meanings of Death*, CAMBRIDGE UNIVERSITY PRESS, Cambridge, 1991, 243 pages, ISBN 0 521 44773 9
— A survey of the interpretation of death in the world's major religions as well as in contemporary scientific and secular belief systems.

Enright, D.J. *The Oxford Book of Death*, OXFORD UNIVERSITY PRESS, Oxford and New York 1983, 353 pages, ISBN 0 19 282013 3
— A collection of hundreds of quotations from the world's great writers and thinkers on topics ranging from the hour of death through to funerals, mourning and resurrection.

Kapleau, Philip *The Wheel of Life and Death*, ANCHOR BOOKS, Doubleday, London, New York, Sydney, 1989, 372 pages, ISBN 0 385 23413 9
— An American Zen Master draws on a wide range of cultural references to offer practical and spiritual answers to existential and contemplative questions about death and the preparation for death. Well written with inspiring quotations, glossary and extensive bibliography.

Long, Barry, *May I speak to you of death*, Audio cassette, THE BARRY LONG FOUNDATION, BCM Box 876 London WC1N 3XX
— Part of this Australian master's *Myth of Life* Series, presenting the facts of death, its purpose and how to mourn.

Nuland, Sherwin *How We Die*, CHATTO AND WINDUS, London, 1993/RANDOM HOUSE, Sydney, Australia, 1994, 278 pages, ISBN 0 7011 6277 5
— An exploration of the medical events that occur when a person dies, stripping away many illusions about death and explaining in detail the processes that take place in the body.

Ring, Kenneth *Heading Toward Omega – In Search of the Meaning of the Near-Death Experience*, QUILL BOOKS, 1985, 348 pages, ISBN 0 688 06268 7
— One of the leading works that explores people's near-death experiences and examines the implications for our assumptions about death, dying and the after-life.

Support for the dying and bereaved

Albery, Nicholas ed. *The Natural Death Handbook*, VIRGIN BOOKS, London, 1993, 222 pages, ISBN 0 86369 687 2
— Written by the leading figures of The Natural Death Centre in the United Kingdom, this is an indispensable compendium of information for carers and families and for people dealing with their own deaths. It presents the fundamental principles of the Natural Death Movement, training for dying, practical care for the dying, green and cheap d-i-y funerals and a manifesto of rights for the dying. Of particular use is *The Good Funeral Guide*, examining facilities throughout the UK with useful references and addresses.

Buckman, Robert *I Don't Know What To Say – How to Help and Support Someone Who is Dying*, MACMILLAN, London, 1988, 247 pages, ISBN 0 333 54035 2
— Sensitive, friendly and practical advice on talking and listening to dying people. Gives helpful insights into the process of dying and detailed suggestions for ways in which carers can be most supportive of their dying loved ones.

DSS (Department of Social Security) *What to do after a death*, Leaflet D49, available free from DSS LEAFLETS UNIT, PO Box 21, Stanmore, Mddx HA7 1AY.

Kübler-Ross, Elisabeth *Living with Death and Dying*, SOUVENIR PRESS, London, 1982, 180 pages, ISBN 0 285 64957
— A distillation of teachings by Dr Kübler-Ross and her colleagues, covering communication with dying people, value of art therapy for the terminally ill, care of dying children and the issue of sudden death.

Lee, Elizabeth *A Good Death*, ROSENDALE PRESS, Premier House, 10 Greycoat Place, London, 1995, 188 pages, ISBN 1 872803 16 4
— A practical guide by a General Practitioner, written in an accessible style and offering a wide range of information on home, hospice and hospital care.

Levine, Stephen *Guided Meditations, Explorations and Healings*, GATEWAY BOOKS, Bath, 1993, 324 pages, ISBN 0 946551 85 5

— A beautifully presented selection of texts that can be used by carers, dying people and others in dealing with pain, intense emotional states, healing, grieving and conscious dying. Each text is introduced with a brief reflection on the issue and both can be used for individual contemplation or with families, groups and in one-on-one healing work.

Levine, Stephen *Who Dies? – An Investigation of Conscious Living and Conscious Dying*, GATEWAY BOOKS, Bath, 1988, 317 pages, ISBN 0 946551 45 6
— A major inspirational work that has helped countless people seeking support and advice in their confrontation with death. Drawing on several spiritual traditions, it offers sensitive insights and advice on befriending the dying, exploring our own emotional response to death and assisting the terminally ill.

Associations and professional support

Internet: see http://www.ubalt.edu/www/bereavement

Age Concern, Astral House, 1268 London Road, London SW16 4ER, offers support and advice including will-writing and funeral arranging.

Ananda Network, 5 Grayswood Point, Norley Vale, Roehampton, London SW15 4BT, provides a Buddhist befriending service for the dying.

Association for Children with Life-threatening Conditions and their families, Institute of Child Health, Royal Hospital for Sick Children, St Michale's Hill, Bristol BS2 8BJ, provides an advice and information service for parents.

Association of Crossroads Care Attendant Schemes, 10 Regents Place, Rugby, Warwickshire CV21 2PN, offers trained carers to give home-bound carers relief.

British Humanist Association, 14 Lambs Conduit Passage, London WC1R 4AH, can provide officiant for non-religious funerals.

Carers National Assocation, 20–25 Glasshouse Yard, London EC1A 4JS, can put carers in touch with local sources of information and support.

The Compassionate Friends, 53 North Street, Bristol BS3 1EN, arranges befriending for bereaved adults.

Crossroads, 10 Regent Place, Rugby, Warwickshire CV21 2PN, has a nationwide network of trained carers who can take over to allow the regular carer to have a break.

Counsel and Care, Twyman House, 16 Bonny Street, London NW1 9PG, maintains a free, confidential and comprehensive advice service for older people, their families and professionals.

CRUSE, 126 Sheen Road, Richmond, Surrey TW9 1UR, offers advice and counselling for the bereaved.

Hospice Information Service, St Christopher's Hospice, 51–59 Lawrie Park Road, Sydenham, London SE26 6DZ, offers a nationwide directory of hospice and palliative care services.

Jewish Bereavement Counselling Service, 1 Cyprus Gardens, London N3 1SP.

Lesbian and Gay Bereavement Project, Vaughan M. Williams Centre, Colindale Hospital, London NW9 5GJ, gives advice on a range of issues, including funerals which are open about the partner.

National Association of Bereavement Services, 20 Norton Folgate, London E1 6DB, offers telephone counselling, advice and comprehensive information, including nearest source of support.

National Black Bereavement Foundation, 25 Bayham St, Camden, London NW1.

The National Death Centre, 20 Heber Road, London NW2 6AA, is a charity which supplies volunteers who visit the homes of those receiving palliative care, to help relieve the carer. It also co-ordinates a network of Green burial grounds (where a tree is planted instead of having a headstone). It publishes a set of forms (Living Will, Death Plan and Advance Funeral Wishes) costing 4 first class stamps; and an information pack on Inexpensive, Green, Family-Organized Funerals (where to get cardboard coffins, addresses of Green burial grounds, etc.), costing 6 first class stamps. Comprehensive and up-do-date listings and advice available. Tel: 0181 208 2853.

Personal Undertakings, PO Box 22, Torquay TQ1 4YJ, assists people who want to organize funerals without the involvement and expense of a funeral director.

Rainbow Trust, Rainbow House, 47 Eastwick Drive, Great Bookham, Leatherhead, Surrey KT23 3PU, supports and cares for children with life-treating conditions and assists their families

Samaritans, 10 The Grove, Slough, Berks. SL1 1QP, or local directory, offering counselling and advice to those contemplating suicide or otherwise affected by it.

Terence Higgins Trust, 52054 Grays Inn Road, London WC1X 8JU, provides advice and support on HIV and AIDS.

Spiritual care for the dying

Neuberger, Julia *Caring for Dying People of Different Faiths*, MOSBY, London (c/o Times Mirror International Publishers, Lynton House, 7–12 Tavistock Square, London WC1H 9LB), 1987, 64 pages, ISBN 0 7234 2154 4
— A sensitive and helpful guide to the practices and beliefs in seven major religions.

Sogyal *The Tibetan Book of Living and Dying*, RIDER, London, 1992, 425 pages, ISBN 0 7126 5437 2
— "What do I hope for from this book? I hope to inspire a quiet revolution in the whole way we look at death and care for the dying, and the whole way we look at life, and caring for the living," writes this Tibetan Rinpoche whose book has been translated into dozens of languages worldwide. Includes detailed instructions on meditation practices at the time of death.

Sogyal *For the Moment of Death*, Audio cassette, RIGPA MEDITATION CENTRE, 330 Caledonian Road, London N1 1BB.
— Advice for the dying and their carers from the author of *The Tibetan Book of Living and Dying* given to an audience of his meditation students.

Complementary therapies

GENERAL

Shreeve, Caroline M. *The Alternative Dictionary of Symptoms and Cures*, CENTURY HUTCHINSON, London, 1987, 504 pages, ISBN 0 7126 1815 5
— A comprehensive listing of medical disorders, explaining the orthodox treatment and alternative remedies. Explains and comments on a considerable range of complementary therapies. An extremely useful reference book to have on hand.

Kaptchuk, Ted and Croucher, Michael *The Healing Arts*, BRITISH BROADCASTING CORPORATION, London, 1986, 175 pages, ISBN 0 563 20447 8
— An open-minded introduction to a wide spectrum of medical systems, addressing fundamental questions such as "What is Illness?", "What effect does the mind have on the body?" and introducing a fascinating range of alternative therapies.

Kaptchuk, Ted *Chinese Medicine – The Web that has no Weaver*, RIDER, London, 1983, 402 pages, ISBN 0 7126 1172 X
— An authoritative introduction for the lay reader to the world's oldest and most extensive medical system, with an excellent general overview of the principles of Chinese Medicine, the meridians and the patterns of energy in the body.

The British Register of Complementary Practitioners, c/o The Institute of Complementary Medicine, PO Box 194, London SE14 1QZ.

ART AND COLOUR THERAPY

Gimbel, Theo *The Book of Colour Healing*, GAIA BOOKS, London, 1994, 128 pages, ISBN 0 671 86857
— Draws on energy theories from India, China and Egypt as well as contemporary research to show how colour can be used in healing.

The British Association of Art Therapists, 13c Northwood Road, London N6 5LT.

AROMATHERAPY

Maxwell-Hudson, Clare *Aromatherapy Massage Book*, DORLING KINDERSLEY, London, 1994, 112 pages, ISBN 0 7513 0140 X
— Basic guide to the fundamental massage techniques and essential oils of aromatherapy. Suitable for people with no previous experience.

Price, Shirley *Aromatherapy for Common Ailments*, GAIA BOOKS, London, 1991, 96 pages, ISBN 1 85675 005 1
— Specific advice on how to apply thirty different essential oils to treat a wide range of ailments.

Aromatherapy Organisations Council, 3 Latymer Close, Braybrooke, Market Harborough, Leicester LE16 8LN.

ENERGY EXERCISES

Lam, Kam Chuen *The Way of Energy*, GAIA BOOKS, London, 1991, 192 pages, ISBN 1 85675 020 5
— A landmark work, presenting the inner workings and recommended practices for the most powerful of all Chi Kung systems, Zhan Zhuang (Standing Like a Tree). Includes advice for use of the system at various stages of life and in relation to illness.

Stand Still Be Fit, Video cassette, CHANNEL 4 TELEVISION, PO Box 4000, London W3 6XJ.

The Zhan Zhuang Chi Kung Research Group UK, 1st Floor, 70 Shaftesbury Avenue, London WC1V 7DF.

HERBALISM AND FLOWER REMEDIES

McIntyre, Anne *Herbs for Common Ailments*, GAIA BOOKS, London, 1992, 96 pages, ISBN 01 85675 055 8
— Shows you how to identify, choose and prepare herbs so that they can be used effectively and safely to relieve symptoms of a range of illnesses and complaints.

Ball, Stephan *Flower Remedies*, BLITZ EDITIONS, BOOKMART LTD, Desford Road, Enderby, Leicester LE9 5AD, 1996, 256 pages, ISBN 1 85605 329 6
— A practical reference book on the use of Dr Bach's flower remedies to balance negative emotional states and so encourage better health.

The Bach Centre, Mount Vernon, Sotwell, Wallingford, Oxon. OX10 0PZ.

The National Institute of Herbal Medicine, 148 Forest Road, Tunbridge Wells, Kent.

MASSAGE

Lidell, Lucinda *The Book of Massage*, EBURY PRESS, London, 1990, 192 pages, ISBN 0 85223 328 0
— A carefully presented guide to both Western and Eastern massage techniques for relieving stress, easing tension and promoting wellbeing. Profusely illustrated for easy use.

Maxwell-Hudson, Clare *The Complete Book of Massage*, DORLING KINDERSLEY, London, 1988, 144 pages, ISBN 0 86318 281 X

Thomas, Sara *Massage for Common Ailments*, GAIA BOOKS, London, 1993, 96 pages, ISBN 1 85675 031 0
— Precise instructions on massage for disorders ranging from headaches and back pain to constipation and chest congestion.

The Massage Institute of Great Britain, 87 Dartmouth Road, London NW2, maintains a register of professionally qualified practitioners.

SHIATSU

Lundberg, Paul *The Book of Shiatsu*, GAIA BOOKS, London, 1992, 192 pages, ISBN 1 85675 060 4

Beresford-Cooke, Carola *Shiatsu Theory and Practice*, CHURCHILL LIVINGSTONE, 1996, 292 pages, ISBN 0 44304 941 6

The Register of the Shiatsu Society, c/o The Shiatsu Society, 5 Foxcote, Wokingham, Berks. RG11 3PG.

SOUND THERAPY

Dewhurst-Maddox, Olivea *Healing with Sound*, GAIA BOOKS, London, 1993, 128 pages, ISBN 1 85675 006 X
— An inspiring guide to the healing art of sound therapy, using the vibrational quality of one's own voice and music to affect the flow of energy in the body and mind.

The Association of Professional Music Therapists, 22 Ermine Street, Caxton, Cambridgeshire CB3 8PQ.

Nutrition

Stanway, Penny *Healing Foods for Common Ailments*, GAIA BOOKS, London, 1995, 96 pages, ISBN 1 85675 017 5
— An up-to-date guide to the medicinal value of foods with a directory of healing food for some 80 ailments.

Van Straten, Michael and Griggs, Barbara *Super Foods*, DORLING KINDERSLEY, London, 1990, 224 pages, ISBN 0 86318 494 4
— Explains how to use foods as medicines, offering clear nutritional guidelines with a list of superfoods that are particularly helpful for a range of conditions, including life-threatening diseases.

The Institute of Complementary Medicine, PO Box 194, London SE14 1QZ, maintains a register of nutritional therapists in the UK.

Stress release

Kirsta, Alix *The Book of Stress Release*. GAIA BOOKS, London, 1986, 192 pages, ISBN 0 7225 2592 3
— A wide-ranging manual on relaxation and stress management techniques, offering step-by-step guidance on mental exercises, physical release and massage to help overcome the debilitating effects of stress.

McCarthy, Merle *Stress Release*, Audio cassette, available from MERLE MCCARTHY, 188 Redlands Road, Penarth, S. Glam. CF6 1QS.

Other useful references and addresses:

The British Acupuncture Association and Register, 34 Alderney Street, London SW1 4EV.

The British Homeopathic Association, 27A Devonshire Street, London W1N 1RJ.

About this book

This book began with a question. "Wouldn't it be useful if there were a book showing how massage, aromatherapy and other complementary health systems could help people who are dying?" It came to mind while I was studying several shelves of health books in the London office of Gaia Books. Sometime later, a major American publisher also asked the same question. Gaia's publisher, Joss Pearson, convened a small team to design and plan exactly such a book, drawing on their years of experience in publishing and the expertise of leading authors and practitioners.

Great emphasis was placed on the design of the book: we wanted to roll back the taboo of talking about death. The book was to have an open, welcoming style. It would invite people to think in fresh ways about their own deaths and encourage them to reach out with care and compassion to their friends and relatives. Hours of time, thoughtfulness and sensitivity were devoted to this by the designer, Bridget Morley, by the artists, Keith Banks and Ann Savage, by the picture researcher, Gill Smith, by the whole team at Aardvark Editorial, Linda Norris, Bryony Allen and Maggie Lythgoe, and by Gaia's Art Director, Patrick Nugent.

Ensuring that the book was well received in the publishing world and sold worldwide was a formidable challenge since we were up against all the traditional fears about discussing death. Joss Pearson was a rock of certainty, enthusiastically assisted by Suzy Boston. In the UK, it was Eleanor Lines who repeatedly rose to the challenge of making the book a publishing reality.

Responsibility for keeping the entire project on track and ensuring that we always struck the right tone rested with the Managing Editor, Pip Morgan, who also provided the meticulous editorial work and fine judgment that was required. His dedicated help was also essential in securing the invaluable contribution of many of the expert consultants.

The book rests principally on the contributions made by those consultants. Brief details about each of them are given on page 190. Many are well-known authors, practitioners, teachers and innovators in their own right. Many have extensive experience of dying people and their carers, working as counsellors, health professionals and educators. In addition, Dame Cicely Saunders, the moving spirit of the modern hospice movement and founder of St Christopher's Hospice in Sydenham, gave illuminating suggestions that are reflected throughout. I am also grateful to the Hesperian Foundation for permission to reproduce the text from *Where There is No Doctor*.

Many other people contributed, knowingly or unknowingly: the practitioners, members and the practice manager, Shirley Sadler, of the Hoxton Health Group in East London; my indefatigable partner, Jane Ward, who helped nurture the project throughout, contributing her own experience as an intensive care nurse, massage therapist and aromatherapist; Pat Fitton and Jean Willson, both of whom assessed the text in light of their own experience of caring for and surviving the deaths of loved ones; Barbara Rae who, while dying, has continued to call for a sea-change in our attitudes; Sue Lumsden who proofread the final draft after undergoing treatment for breast cancer; Kim and Hilary Lovelace, whose own wisdom and collection of books and tapes on death and dying were most helpful; Hilary de Boerr who provided material on natural childbirth; Maggie Draper at Trinity Hospice, London; Jan Bleckman, Debbie Coats, Judy Holder, Maggie Lewis, Jane Lindsay and John Steer of The Shambhala Centre, London; Patti Whaley who so willingly helped the research into Christian perspectives on death; Eric Prokosch, Gillian Hoffmann, Jack Griffiths and Aladdin Hassanali who helped track down Arabic, Hebrew and Russian texts; Jim and Steve McCarthy whose encouragement and own encounters with death persistently reminded me that such a book was needed; Franca Sciuto, her family and friends, all of whom suffered great pain after the violent death of her daughter, Gabriella, and for all of whom a book such as this may be helpful in the future.

As the work unfolded, it became clear that its approach had to extend beyond the application of the therapies alone. The teachers and authors who influenced the fuller shape of the book are too numerous to name (many are included in the Resources pages so that others can benefit) and extend back to the two individuals who very first taught me the importance of understanding death: my parents. Following in the tradition to which they introduced me, I am deeply indebted to the teachings which I have attended by His Holiness the XIVth Dalai Lama, Khenpo Tsultrim Gyampso Rinpoche, Dzigar Kongtrol Rinpoche and to the unsurpassable kindness, generosity and compassion of Sakyong Mipham Rinpoche.

None of this would have been possible at this point in my life without the incomparable care and instruction of Master Lam Kam Chuen, whose wisdom, learning and gentle discipline have guided me for over a decade.

When my now dead friend and colleague, John Cooper, asked me to find him a book on dying well, I was unable to locate one. Here, at last, is what I would have liked to have found for him.

RICHARD REOCH

THE AUTHOR

Richard Reoch is a specialist in Oriental and complementary health systems in which the ageing and dying are treated with great respect. He is a member of the Register of the Shiatsu Society of the United Kingdom and a practitioner in the Hoxton Health Group for the over-60s in East London. He has been a Tai Chi Chuan instructor at the Royal College of Nursing and the European School of Osteopathy and currently leads Tai Chi classes at City and Islington College in London. In 1991 he was invited by Master Lam Kam Chuen to collaborate with him to produce *The Way of Energy*, which opened up the Zhan Zhuang system of Chi Kung to the West. Born in Canada in 1948, he grew up in a Buddhist family and was for many years a senior official of Amnesty International, working on behalf of the tortured and with the families of the dead and the "disappeared" throughout the world.

THE CONSULTANTS

Stefan Ball works with the trustees of the Bach Flower Centre as a consultant. He is the author of *Flower Remedies* and *Bach Flower Remedies for Men*.

Carola Beresford-Cooke is one of the founders of The Shiatsu College in London and author of *Massage for Healing and Relaxation*, *Acupressure* and the comprehensive Churchill Livingstone manual, *Shiatsu Theory and Practice*. She was a major contributor to Gaia Books' *The Book of Massage*.

Olivea Dewhurst-Maddox is a professional practitioner of the art of healing through sound, working in colleges, schools and prisons in the UK. She is the author of *Healing with Sound* published by Gaia Books.

Kenneth J. Doka is Professor of Gerontology at the College of New Rochelle and senior consultant to the Hospice Foundation of America. He has written or edited five books on grief and loss including *Disenfranchised Grief: Recognizing Hidden Sorrow*. Currently, Dr Doka serves as chair of the International Work Group on Death, Dying and Bereavement.

Theo Gimbel researches and teaches internationally on the impact of colour. He is the author of Gaia Books' *The Book of Colour Healing*.

James Kuykendall is a bereavement therapist specializing in child and adolescent trauma. Formerly at Charing Cross Hospital London, he pioneered training in the UK on the psychological needs of clients with HIV/AIDS and now lectures worldwide.

Master Lam Kam Chuen is a leading authority on the Chinese health systems of Zhan Zhuang Chi Kung and Tai Chi, as well as a practitioner of Traditional Chinese Medicine. He is the author of *The Way of Energy*, *Step-by-Step Tai Chi*, and *The Feng Shui Handbook* all published by Gaia Books.

Clare Maxwell-Hudson is the founder of the Clare Maxwell-Hudson School of Massage in London, Director of the Institute of Health Sciences and teaches at the Royal College of Nursing. She was a contributor to *The Book of Massage* (Gaia Books) and author of *The Complete Book of Massage* and *Aromatherapy Massage Book*.

Anne McIntyre is a director of the National Institute of Medical Herbalism. She is the author of Gaia Books' *The Complete Woman's Herbal* and *Herbs for Common Ailments*.

Betty O'Gorman is the Head of Physiotherapy at St Christopher's Hospice, London, and has been instrumental in the development of physiotherapy in palliative care. As a founder member of the Association of Chartered Physiotherapists in Oncology and Palliative Care, she has represented it on the Professional Committee of the National Council for Hospice and Specialist Palliative Care Services.

Shirley Price is the founder of the Shirley Price School of Aromatherapy with branches in Ireland, Norway, the UK and USA. She is the author of *Practical Aromatherapy* and *Aromatherapy for Common Ailments* (Gaia Books).

Ellen Zinner is a licensed psychologist and certified grief therapist who has worked as an educator, researcher, author and clinician in the fields of loss and grief in the United States for over two decades. She is past president of the Association for Death Education and Counseling.

PUBLISHER'S ACKNOWLEDGEMENTS

Photographs Robert Ayres, p.15. THE BRIDGEMAN ART LIBRARY, p.179 British Museum, London, p.182 Oriental Museum, Durham University. BRUCE COLEMAN COLLECTION, p.50 Hans Reinhard, p.102 Erwin & Peggy Bauer, p.145 Stephen J. Krasemann, p.158 Felix Labhardt, p.175 Jules Cowan. SCIENCE PHOTO LIBRARY, p.22 Alex Bartel, p.99 George Bernard, p.123 Space Telescope Science Institute/NASA, p.126 George Ranalli, p.169 Simon Fraser. South American Pictures, p.163 Robert Francis. TONY STONE, p.41 Randy Wells, p.141 James F. Housel. Winnipeg Art Gallery, p.21 Flight of the Shaman (1970) Public Trustee for the Northwest Territories, estate of Jessie Oonark. ZEFA PICTURES LTD, p.12 Steve Prezant, p.31 Zefa Pictures UK, pp.32, 33 Zefa Pictures UK, p.35 Don James, p.118 Ch. Gupton.

Illustrations by Keith Banks, Ann Savage and Bridget Morley. Grateful thanks to Frances Donnelly, Marion Gaze and Michael Posen for modelling.

Quotation on pages 32–3 *Where There Is No Doctor: A Village Health Care Handbook* by David Werner with Carol Thuman and Jane Maxwell, published by the Hesperian Foundation, PO Box 1692, Palo Alto, CA. USA.

INDEX

www.ingramcontent.com/pod-product-compliance
Lightning Source LLC
Chambersburg PA
CBHW080758300326
41914CB00055B/932